the parasite

i
have
traveled
the
world

on
the
backs
of
people

whose
lives
are
held
together

by
the
wars
they
fight

– jpl

Contents

Acknowledgements

To the many people whose stories appear in *The Pocket Guide*, my friends and mentors from around the world who exemplify daily the courage we need for facing the challenges of violent conflict, I am honored and inspired by you and the communities where you live and lead. Thank you!

The Pocket Guide would not have reached publication without the extraordinary support and help from Laura Webber, who has accompanied this process at every level from the beginning. To my close colleagues Melanie Greenberg, Tom Glaisyer, and Krista Tippet who have consistently offered excellent feedback, encouragement, and ideas on how best to situate this book, I am deeply grateful. I have benefitted from clear insights from a range of wise advisers from Humanity United, Democracy Fund, and the Ford Foundation who have offered both strategic ideas and technical expertise as the final draft emerged. For this, special thanks are due for the contributions of Michelle Barsa, Hillary Pennington, and Beth Kim. The deep editing detail from Andrew Donlan improved the entire text, as did the keen visual eye of Marta Ribeiro on the cover design and formatting.

I have a list too long to mention of people who read early versions and provided great advice. I am especially thankful for the conversations with Amanda Ripley and John Avlon — their suggestions and encouragement were key. My heartfelt gratitude goes to my home organization, Humanity United, and the brilliant team of the Peacebuilding portfolio.

Finally, I am blessed beyond words for the love, patience, and grounding from Wendy and our wider family. In so many ways this book was written for our grandchildren, all of them.

Foreword

Introduction

Three inquiries have been populating my inbox.

Do you think we are being pulled into a civil war here in the United States?

In your experience, what international case of civil war seems to parallel what we face here at home?

And the third one that kept coming: *What can I do?*

They land on my desk because over four decades I have worked in settings of armed conflict, both with local communities most impacted by the sustained violence and in support of national negotiations seeking to end the violence.

These questions beg for comparison and prediction. Neither is easy and rarely appropriate.

I have worked with local communities and national leaders in places like Northern Ireland, the Basque Country, Ethiopia, Somalia, West Africa, South Sudan, Nicaragua, Colombia, Mexico, Myanmar, the Philippines, Nepal, and Tajikistan. These settings taught me about suffering and frustration and toxicity. They also taught me about courage and imagination and persistence.

In most places I have worked people do not describe their situation with the phrase *civil war*. They struggle to find language. Local references and vernacular become shorthand: The Troubles. The Conflict. The Revolution. The Revolt. The Insurgency.

In many regards, this reveals an important truth. Every context is *sui generis*. Few sweeping generalizations pass the test of time. Too often, comparisons serve outside analysis more than internal processes. And no matter how specific a general theory of comparison develops, exceptions always abound.

At the same time, in all these locations, curiosity reigns. People want to know what others have done in similar circumstances. It seems the nature of humanity to wonder if we are alone, or if there are people who share our dilemmas.

Across my experiences one simple observation persists: Once unleashed, open violence creates a torrent of toxicity and harm resistant to change.

Repeated cycles of open violence continuously add new layers of suffering to historic trauma rising from and contributing to structural violences, such as inequality and exclusion, in the many forms they have taken in different contexts.

To say the least, this gives me pause when I receive questions about a civil war in the United States.

The Pause

In the United States, when we hear *civil war*, we imagine something like the 1860s when our country traversed a devastating state vs. state war for which there was never full repair, reconstruction, and reconciliation. We continue to face powerful legacies of intergenerational trauma connected to the theft of indigenous life and land and the wounds suffered from slavery. It is highly unlikely we will return to the type of interstate war experience of our nation's past.

There is no one comparable case from the international locations of armed conflict mentioned above. And yet, it is also true that none of them would have predicted what eventually emerged in their own settings — this unraveling of conflict into sustained open violence over decades.

And this is what gives me pause: The unraveling that leads from toxic polarization to outright violence is far more prevalent and dangerous than we fully understand.

While our legacy of American exceptionalism mostly scoffs at international comparisons, this does not exempt us from the patterns and dynamics that unleash what none of us wants for our children — the curse of wide-spread violence.

I urge a national pause.

To be precise, we need a critical threshold of local people to take a pause and look carefully at what is happening in our own back-yards, in the pockets where we live.

We see the red flags. They pepper our news and social media daily. Recent events of open violence during an election period only raise the concern further.

Consider some facts on the ground, factors that will not be resolved by the outcome of an election.

While we in the United States live in a highly pluralistic country, we have long contested the meaning of belonging. Today, that contestation has become embroiled in identity divides infused with a sense of desperation: If *they* prevail, *we* will not survive.

We have the most porous, tolerant laws governing the right to bear arms of any country in the world. We refer to coordinated civilian armed groups as militias, a term etched into our constitution. We read reports and polls indicating that armed violence is increasingly justified and legitimate to protect "us" against the threat of "them" — all of whom happen to be our fellow citizens.

We are watching in real time as the legitimacy of our governing institutions and our basic avenues of political participation, like elections, increasingly face questions, challenges, and threats.

Perhaps most significantly, while we argue about the meaning and interpretation of our constitution, we pay little attention to the erosion of our social contract.

We need this pause, at once both local and national, to be sufficient in depth for us to reflect on at least two things.

First, what can we learn by stepping back to observe the social dynamics of toxic polarization that take us down the path to further legitimize violence?

I believe one avenue for exploring this question comes by observing how those propensities manifest in settings of full-blown armed conflict.

Second, what we can learn from everyday people who creatively reversed those destructive dynamics while facing repeated cycles of violence and war?

To paraphrase a famous presidential line, our imperative is not to ascertain *what others will do for us,* but *what we will do for each other where we live.* This asks us to live into the most basic principle of our social contract: That we in the United States can forge politics without violence.

Preparing to Read

By official titles, I am both a practitioner and a scholar of peace-building and a professional mediator. Some call me professor. I take it as a title of respect, though at times from the trenches of deep conflict, I acknowledge legitimate doubts about the seemingly remote and at times lofty intellectualism of academic venues.

I have worked extensively in settings of vicious conflict and sat through countless hours, time and again over decades, of seemingly hopeless conversations. This vocation has gifted a lifetime of both challenges and inspiration, but most importantly it afforded me a hard-won experience in finding practical ways out of violent conflict.

I organized this book in ten brief chapters. For what it is worth, my reflections emerge from what I have learned from living and working in places where extraordinarily courageous changemakers kept finding ways to shift away from the dynamics of open violence toward the practices of social healing.

The organization of *The Pocket Guide* is simple.

In each chapter I describe a prevalent, critical dynamic or two that must be faced if moving away from violence will not only become possible, but will endure over time.

In each chapter, again drawing from experience, I offer stories of everyday people who, across their differences, jointly resisted cycles of violence in surprising ways.

A pocket guide is never a comprehensive guide. Don't expect one.

Many of the people I learned from spent lifetimes in the heart of these conflicts. Most were born into a protracted war. I found very few who suggested quick fixes or miracle recipes. In fact, they were suspicious of anyone who did. What they offered were their stories.

Many authors have rightly adopted a focus on historical and political analyses of civil wars, offering solutions in the form of top-down policies, strategies for negotiation, or official guidance for institutions.

The Pocket Guide offers something different by exploring the way ordinary people resisted and countered the patterns of violence where they worked and lived. What they innovated speaks directly to the deep pragmatics of an enduring social contract.

In the broad landscape of facing down a civil war, each of us matters.

The quality of how we relate and stay in relationship across difference matters.

And every small act to heal our tattered social fabric matters.

CHAPTER 1

Watch Your Pockets
When the sporadic becomes sustained

Listen, saying my name requires me to cite my lineage.
Our lineage is like a post office box for you. It will always
trace you home. Everybody is the cousin of somebody, and
everybody knows your local post address. You might call it a
civil war, but it's all local and it's all changing. Everyday.
You have to know the "sub-sub" in the subclan thing in this
mess of a fight.

Personal conversation with a Somali friend,
Mogadishu, 1991

Few civil wars initiate nationally.

While political rhetoric in capital cities has often been very heated, my experience over the past four decades suggests that armed conflict unfolds locally.

Exceptions abound.

We could start with famous assassinations, such as Archduke Franz Ferdinand prior to WW1, or the deaths of Rwandan and Burundian presidents in the airline catastrophe of 1994. We have just recently seen that symbolic targeting of high-level political figures cannot be ruled out in the United States. History tells us such acts can emerge as a strategy to trigger wider conflict.

I return to experience, which suggests the need to carefully observe and respect what is emergent at the local level. The consistent pattern behind sustained armed conflict employs violence to exert fear and dominate power in local geographies. Control is sought over places and people.

By *pockets* I refer to a localized geography where armed groups seek to establish and solidify a controlling presence.

For example, after the signing of the peace agreement in Nepal, research showed that more than one hundred new regionally-based armed groups emerged — a clear sign that access to political inclusion required local armed control.

A core and recurring strategy, particularly when formerly dominant groups cohere around a sense of decline in their agency, is that they will seek to exert power where they feel they have greatest access and potential for domination. That often starts locally.

These local dynamics give rise to different terminology around the world. Al Qaeda refers to *cells*. *Zulos* in the Basque region, *territories* in Colombia, and *interface communities* in Belfast are all examples of organizing and engaging in pockets of contested territory.

In early phases, presence and actions of these groups were perceived from a national lens as appalling, but they were framed as requiring some form of policing response. In many places the contested geographies were remote, the security response slow and weak in capacity, frequently under threat or even compromised.

Facing increased presence of armed actors, citizens in local communities experience a vacuum of public security, which in turn is filled by the militias. A significant number of these groups make the case that they are, in fact, the only source that assures safety.

Almost to a setting, the armed group activity is initially perceived as *sporadic violence*. I use the term sporadic because it reflects the perception that the armed groups actions are an aberration, not the norm. At national levels, I commonly heard references to these events described in this way: *These things happen, but it is not who we are.*

In fact, national political leadership tends to downplay the pocket challenges. Perhaps they do this because acknowledging that a wider pattern exists would project political weakness and a lack of formal, institutional capacity. In my experience, by the time officials publicly acknowledge the pattern, it is well after the groups are established.

In most places where this pocket dynamic emerges, local armed groups hide in plain sight. But they hide. They take great care to develop closely guarded identities replete with *noms-de-guerre*, secretive communication, quiet accumulation of weapons, and clandestine coordination. Focusing on the local also affords reduced resistance and creates more specific boundaries — a territory that can be controlled.

Over time *pocket* patterns emerge.

First and most significant, at some point violent activity transitions from *sporadic* to *sustained*.

Violent events become less isolated and cross local boundaries. They slowly unveil a stitching. People behind the events have mostly hidden connections that shroud their networking yet create highly effective and decentralized infrastructures of support.

Throughout these settings, the laws of extreme polarization kick in. In deeply divided societies, impulses for counteraction and retaliation set in motion a cycle of violent reactivity that takes on a life of its own. Sociologists refer to this as *reciprocal causation*: Each act creates a catalyst for reaction, until the back and forth of counterresponses create ongoing cycles that function *independent* of their originating causes.

In many settings, one of the keys to achieving a foothold while hiding in plain sight comes with repeated incidents of harm that slowly normalize violence. Of note, no single moment or act marks the exact shift from sporadic to sustained violence.

A second pocket dynamic that accompanies the increasingly open presence of armed groups is their focus on achieving at least tacit compliance by way of fear and direct confrontation. This is often done through the targeting of local leaders who are perceived as a threat and by way of performative violence in the local community. Here we note two different but clearly connected goals for dealing with adversaries and enemies: Enforce local submission *within* the pocket and directly target symbolic enemies *outside* that have national visibility.

Within the pocket we find that actions against perceived resistance and adversaries start by calling people out, social shaming, and deterring resistance by suppressing those who may openly protest. *Internal adversaries* often suffer direct violence and these performative acts send a message to others to fall in line and stay silent.

The violence also focuses on highly visible attacks against national symbols and well-known adversaries *external* to the local pocket. Striking examples of these two include assassinations of local leaders and the kidnapping of high-profile national leaders in Colombia. Or, as was the case during the Troubles, kneecapping as social sanction in Belfast and the bombing of symbolic national and international economic targets.

Supported by a narrative of grievance, this violence is almost always justified as a last resort to protect threats to "our way of life," "our identity," or "our very survival." Some of these may well be grievances that are shared by local communities. Armed groups have an astute awareness of the local emotional landscape of alienation and use it consistently to justify and legitimate their behavior. A complex mix of fear, control, and active violence often leads to submission, tacit support, and reluctance to openly oppose the armed groups.

Another key pocket factor sets out to create conditions where sporadic violence provides a foothold for a sustained "legitimate" presence without this presence being fully noticed, especially nationally, until it is too late to halt its momentum.

Civil wars do not appear overnight from the top-down. They require a strong local base and an equally robust stitching between pockets that support the infrastructure for later growth.

How can these dynamics be resisted? How can the transition from sporadic to sustained violence be faced down?

Part of the answer may lie in the experiences of people who found ways to respond. Time and again, the shift began with *pocket imagination*. Local people came together, shared what they knew, combined their networks, and developed practical responses.

Consider the Women of Wajir who, facing decades of clan-based militia violence in the border areas of Somalia and Kenya, started with three ideas.

Paraphrasing their recollection of early conversation:

A few of us from different clans sat together to see what we knew. We asked each who we knew, so that we could think about the connections we had. We were not many when we started, but we were from different subclans. We then decided what we could propose as a first step, what specific action could we do together that we all cared about.

They knew the local market had become unsafe, which meant their food and basic economy was at risk.

They recognized that their social connections cut across subclans and could reach to their families, local leaders, youth, and businesspeople. They chose to focus on one concrete need they all shared: How to help make the market safe and accessible to anyone from any subclan. They built an informal network of women across clans to monitor the market to ensure that any person from any subclan could buy and sell without being harmed.

Creating a secure market was an audacious first step.

But they forged ahead. They gathered regularly to share learning and insights. Over time they created a civilian-based disarmament movement. Economic development initiatives followed, focused on jobs for youth. They engaged elders and religious leaders to open cross-clan conversations. They eventually negotiated with security forces and Kenyan parliamentarians. By their perseverance, they contributed to transforming the level of violence, if not ending the war in their region.

Systems of violence often result in paralysis, creating a mindset that presumes solutions can only come from outside and from above. Prevalent is the sense that accountability, protection, and change will only emerge from a more powerful level of authority or sanction.

Evidence from settings of protracted violence suggests the opposite bears out. Some of the most surprising processes of change came about as people tapped their own imagination and trusted their local knowledge and networks. In essence, people met pocket violence with a pocket response.

Kenneth Boulding recommends this sort of imagination as a theory of change: *If it exists, it is possible.*[1] The shift begins with access and dialogue. People move away from *sustained violence* by strategically creating the capacity to *sustain dialogue*, a phrase former Under Secretary of State Harold Saunders employed in dozens of local settings.

What might be the keys?

Start where you have access. Don't wait. Take responsibility. Create the surprise of unlikely spaces of dialogue, engagement, and joint action across divisions. Find accessible, immediate, and practical steps that appeal to a wider group and then bring into reality the very outcome pursued: Learning to work together *with* differences *without* violence.

While stopping a full-blown civil war requires reducing toxicity among visible political leaders, preventing a war requires a web of people who sustain meaningful conversations and relationships across divides.

The first step is the courage to start.

If the Women of Wajir offer a path forward, it may be this. See who you know. Find the rare few, unlikely conversation partners who are willing to sit together. See what you know. See what you can propose together. Choose one joint practical step that can make a difference where you live.

Ask for accountability from high level officials, but not miracles. Focus the imagination and responsibility you can take together on what is practical and immediately accessible. Then, never stop aspiring to reach the next level of engaged relationship.

CHAPTER 2

Hiding In Plain Sight
Watch the spider's silk, not the lone wolf

*The spider makes what for a human would be very complex
calculations: "How big is the open space? How much silk do
I have? What attachment points are available?" Spiders are
not little automatons making the same thing over and over.
They're flexible. And they're not stupidly flexible; they're
smart flexible...Life in the web, as one spider scientist put it,
means "hanging your butt in the breeze"...hiding in plain
sight is thus among the spider's chief preoccupations.*

Richard Coniff's conversation with arachnologist
Bill Eberhard, 2001

Among the many challenges of armed conflict is its inherent capacity to replicate over time. Once unleashed, efforts to end open
violence fail more often than they succeed. Armed responses function like a computer's default button — a return to *normal* becomes
a return to *violence*. Particularly in places where armed conflict fes-
ters for long periods of time, the perplexing question remains:
How do cycles of open violence become so intractable and resilient?

Resilience refers to this systemic regenerative capacity to *bounce
back*, time and again. Resiliency is often observed as outcome.
Less understood are the innate qualities that make, in this case,

15

a violent regeneration possible. In settings of protracted conflict, particularly those that replicate in open societies, better understanding requires attentive observation: We must probe for what is hidden in plain sight.

Coniff's conversation with Eberhard, aptly titled "Deadly Silk,"[2] offers a first clue: *Pay more attention to how the stitching coheres than to the stitcher.*

Public narratives about armed conflict and civil wars — as they appear in story, journalism, and the now omnipresent worlds of social media — fall prey to significantly unproductive habits: They prioritize a focus on personalities over understanding process, and place far more attention on sensational events than on exploring repeating patterns.

While mainstream public attention is placed on lone wolves, I learned to focus on the relational context required to sustain armed conflict. The bounce-back for this violence will always be found in the hidden web and the relationships and stitching needed to both create and make it possible.

The importance of a spider as a metaphor for probing the nature of a civil war is not in the spider itself, but in its strategy of traversing space, three aspects of which stand out.

First, laying silk for an orb web, the spider relies on the power of anchor points, often located at the far reaches of the space it seeks to cover.

Second, silk laying requires the spider to travel and circulate. Spiders achieve their goal by constantly moving around the space, leaving threads where they travel that create and strengthen individual hubs while also building the whole of the web. This requires not just moving from the center to the periphery and back, but more importantly, moving across expanses at the far margins of the web. The genius lies in the capacity to connect the whole web while assuring that different areas within it will continue to function even if other parts are destroyed.

Third, silk laying unfolds permanently. It is as if the web is in constant development because the goal is not the finalizing of the web as a static outcome. Adaptive flexibility continuously connects and often rebuilds a web with new forms that emerge to adapt to changing conditions — all assure the purpose of the web within the space: To survive.

Armed groups emergent in open societies face a similar challenge of how to sustain their illicit operations while hiding in plain sight. People, weapons, plans, and communication are in a constant but covert adaptation and flow.

Illicit trafficking and armed engagement in Mexico, Colombia, the Northern and Golden Triangles, and Northern Ireland during the Troubles all share some of the aforementioned important features: Anchor points, adaptation, concealment, corridors, strategic hubs, and decentralized connectivity. These critical features weave together in ways that powerfully support why violent patterns repeat.

It is important to consider where attention tends to be focused when the goal is for the infrastructure that supports armed conflict to be sustained over time.

Less attention is paid to owning geography as classic versions of land battles, while prioritized focus is placed on assuring the viability of *corridors* and *trustworthiness* of hubs.

Less attention is paid to institutionalizing services while primary attention is focused on constant and flexible adaptation of how to achieve the delivery of the *goods*, or in this case, the *bads* like weapons or drugs.

Less attention is paid to military victory than to the propagation, this purpose to spread and sustain. This is why cells, not centralization, remain the key organizing feature: Each independent while each links to wider purpose.

Here we also find the connection between violent armed conflict and how it dovetails with toxic polarization: They both result in political paralysis.

Social toxicity often rises on and fuels messages of fear. Increased fear elevates and energizes more zealous political leadership. What was once considered extreme now becomes normalized in the mainstream.

At the same time, fear and toxicity bolster the view that violence is needed to protect *us* from *them*, to protect our way of life and security.

Over time, toxic polarization mixed with violence create conditions by which political process and governance become thick and slow. Institutional responsiveness to basic needs becomes, and certainly is perceived to be, less and less effective and trustworthy. In turn, this reinforces the rising view that public institutions and functionaries have declining legitimacy. These conditions diminish trust, not only across social and political divides as people seek who to blame for the lack of response to their grievances, but also weaken the basic social contract needed for public service to function.

We return to the key point: Toxic polarization and violence paralyze politics and destroy trust.

While the deadly silk of armed conflict builds corridors for re-sources, perhaps the greater impact emerges with how the overall approach shapes a defining narrative that must be faced by local communities, a narrative that weaves a number of elements in a powerful story line.

Trust nothing from the outside.

Trust us because we are local, and our armed presence will take care of your security.

If you cannot trust us, know that you should fear us.

Wood-painted signs on a post that went up at the edge of numer-ous *veredas*, the small rural towns throughout Medio Magdalena in Colombia, might not at first glance even catch the attention of an outsider.

Posted: *You are welcome. No guns allowed in town.*

Half a world away a similar effort afforded civilian protection in numerous places in Mindanao, the Philippines, where raging divi-sions between Muslims and Christians persisted. People during armed conflict began to advocate for and define peace zones.[3]

Peace zones might seem an unlikely way to face local militias and armed groups in the midst of a war. While the primary questions raised have focused on whether these zones make a difference, this may prevent us from perceiving a key to change: How everyday people begin to stitch joint action to stop violence. A declared and negotiated peace zone represents a pocket of resistance to the dy-namics of armed conflict, a remarkable case of improbable positive deviance amid open violence.

To understand how peace zones emerge we must appreciate two mindsets that inspire such bold and imaginative resistance.

The first is the mindset of *enough-is-enough*; the second is the *grandmother's imagination*. How they stimulate resistance merits exploration. Just as the actions of perpetrators of violence tend to be hidden, the contexts of conversations that support coming together to resist are rarely visible to wider public awareness.

Living through decades of repeated violence often builds from and back to a long gaze, the kind a grandparent may have that looks back across a lifetime and forward to the well-being of their grandchildren. For those in Medio Magdalena, this led to great clarity about the practical simplicity of purpose: *Today we will take a step to end these cycles of violence. We do not want this violence to be our legacy of harm to yet another generation.*

At some point, enough-is-enough connects with an imagination that our immediate community and the future well-being our grandchildren's lives are embedded in a *web of relationships* that ultimately include the well-being of our enemy's grandchildren.

What do we find as hidden stitching in this facing down of violence?

In the case of Medio Magdalena, it started with a few folks who formed part of the Association of Workers and Campesinos (ATCC). The association had a startling birth rising from the need to confront the proposal of a local paramilitary commander who demanded they arm themselves with his free offer of guns and to join his ranks as a civilian militia. Most surprising was not just their refusal to join him or leave the region, but their absolute commitment to reject violence.

As they were forming an association, they needed some basic guiding principles and a quota to join their organization. They decided their quota would not ask for an annual fee but rather sought conviction. Membership required commitment to simple and profound phrases: *We choose to die before we kill. We have no enemies. We will negotiate with everyone.*

These few words represented the provocative principle that led to the wooden signs at the edge of villages. The *campesinos* up and down the Carare River had faced armed groups in their region for two decades. They came in waves of varied affiliations and persuasions. The actions that emerged from their principles required the social courage to risk engagement and the art of persuasion. Both start with a grandmother's imagination emergent from the conviction that enough had in fact been enough.

While a literal example of a grandmother's imagination is described in situations like the Women of Wajir or the extraordinary movement of women in Liberia captured in the movie *Pray the Devil Back to Hell*,[4] we find the same imagination among the *campesinos* in rural Magdalena.

Those who incorporate the *enough-is-enough* mindset and *grand-mother's imagination* adopt quite a different outlook on life: *We refuse to bequeath the harms of this toxic violent conflict to yet another generation.*

This unique vision of the future, while simple, is also profound. It spawns a different, more hopeful, trajectory for society.

The grandmother's imagination offers two surprising ways to transcend the vicious pull of violence.

The first envisions a broad view of collective well-being that refuses to fall into the trap of dehumanization. The second, understands *collective* as a daily reminder that humanity shares a common future, even with our enemies. We are ultimately tied together.

This understanding of generational well-being requires that we learn how to bring dignity to all relationships — a shift in mindset beyond the trap of narrow and incurious demands that only see the world as defined by us or them.

Relationships that see beyond eternal enmity always expand the time horizon. At essence, this imagination turns toward curiosity about and willingness to nurture dignified relationships across divides as both immediate need and longer-term purpose. This pursuit of dignity across divides opens the pathway and offers a guiding horizon of humanizing the conflict that includes rearing respect for others while seeking repair, change, and social healing.

Rearing respect may seem an odd verb. But rearing well-being, healing, and the courage to face down violence — this vocational impulse of what a grandmother hopes for her grandchildren — offers a window into the shift of what hides in plain sight: Breaking toxicity starts with openness to notice, reflect on, and nurture dignity in relationships beyond narrowly defined binaries.

Change always starts with imagination about the web you live in and your place in it. The question it continuously poses: Can you find ways to notice that your web, the one that traces to your grandchildren, includes the grandchildren of your enemy?

CHAPTER 3

The Holy Grail of Grievance

*I just have one question: Why do you think violence does
not work? And before you answer, let me tell you a story.*

Loyalist paramilitary commander, Maze Prison,
Northern Ireland, 1993

I have sat for many hours listening to frustrated, angry people in
the middle of fighting urgent and slow wars across generations.

This kind of sit requires patient ears and an unhurried tongue.

Over time, I have learned to focus on the person and concentrate
on the specifics of their story. The concentration is required because the stories are always long and can weave centuries in a single
sentence. Often these stories repeat a basic plot: *We have been den-
igrated and humiliated. Humiliation and violence against us have
created irreparable harm. The humiliators are alive among us. If they
continue, we will, as a people, disappear.*

Donna Hicks refers to these as the experiences that affront basic
dignity.[5] This lived disrespect nurtures the driving root that feeds
deep conflict.

23

Over time I have found that if I am not fully attentive in the conversation, I can easily lose track of where in history, and in whose history, I am located. It is too easy to let my mind roam to other people or contexts, to other conversations where the same grievances were expressed from other sides of the conflict. And if the mind roams to facts or contestation, in that moment it can no longer hold the humanity, the lived experience of the storyteller.

This seemed especially true moving from H-Block to H-Block to H-Block, from one paramilitary conversation to the next, in the Maze Prison in Northern Ireland. The commander cited above seemed to have these two concerns in mind when he spoke: The more open argument about why violence was justified and the less visible feeling about whether our presence in his cell was to understand or judge.

In all conflicts a holy grail of grievance exists. The key is to understand the dynamics of how the grail becomes holy enough to justify violence.

My experience suggests it begins with feeling invisibilized, of sensing and living with the slow burn of what is experienced as humiliation in the form of not being seen, recognized, and acknowledged. When humiliation fans into open outrage, the potential for violence rises sharply.

Deep grievance always carries imagination of the seed that justifies violence. *It no longer matters. Nobody sees us. Nobody cares about us. Nobody listens.*

Then there is nothing left.

In my years of conversations in settings of open violence, I have rarely heard someone describe armed response as their first or preferred choice. Violence is described as *what good people must do to* protect themselves from evil people or harmful systems. Violence is the alternative that *they* have forced *us* to choose.

As philosopher Bruno Bettelheim put it: *Violence is the choice of the person who can imagine no other option.*[6]

Grievance travels a long passageway storied with portraits of heroes and demons, lost loved ones, humiliation, and exclusion. Perhaps most significant is this feeling of being invisibilized, present but not seen. Vlamik Volkan framed the narrative of grievance as the ways that *chosen traumas* and *chosen glories* cohere around identity and the significance of who we are.[7]

I have learned three things about deep grievance.

First, grievance remembers with laser precision the life of harms we have suffered. At the same time, grievance-as-narrative lives in the borderlands of incuriosity and forgetfulness about the suffering we have caused others.

Second, grievance evades responsibility. Always. It fashions two escape hatches: *Defend.* And. *Blame.*

Deep grievance walks hand-in-hand with the potential for violence. It lives with the permanent gnawing feeling that everything is now on the line. It is so painful that it goes unquestioned: Survival *is* at stake.

When survival is at risk a *holiness of purpose* emerges, precisely because the end is always proximate. This is in part why political rhetoric appealing to fear has such power: It always reinforces the most extreme view that we are near extinction.

Third, in the storied passageway of grievance, it is always the *feelings* that matter, not the *facts.*

This may be why grievance never listens beyond its own pain. And why holy grievance has the feel of holy war.

Grievance becomes *holy* if its umbilical attachment remains fixed and fixated on the feeling of ultimate survival. We have arrived at the *all or nothing* moment. And only one option remains: Disappear or respond with violence.

Curious in all this is how the reality of existential survival sustains across decades and generations once violence is unleashed. The average timeframe for how long armed conflicts endures is at least a decade. The Troubles speak of three decades; Colombia and the Sudans have faced armed violence across half-centuries.

The moment of ultimate survival transfers into the too often unnoticed imprint of intergenerational trauma. In turn, the outrage becomes purer, the justification for violence stronger, and the lament thick as ash in places where wars have lasted across three or more generations.

Emerging from the parish meeting hall after a long afternoon conversation, I still recall the warmth on my face from the late afternoon sun.

We waved to the last of the sixty some *campesinos* who had just shared their experiences of unspeakable violence. It is never easy to recount years of suffering in your designated few minutes with so many others around the circle carrying the same weight on their hearts. But that is what the people in the Santander region encircling San José de Miranda, Colombia, had experienced. We had spent a day with sixty of the more than six hundred widows and orphans Father Rafa attended to on weekly basis in his parish.

In an armed conflict that had lasted a half century, the youngest person around that circle represented the third generation of children born to open violence. Their stories that day had left me emotionally drained and shiver-cold. Maybe that's why the warmth of the sun sticks as a memory.

After too many bodies and killings had accumulated in his parish, Father Rafael Cárdenas Ortiz made the decision to find and talk directly with militia leaders. When I asked him how he approached the commanders who had caused such suffering, especially when they would first meet him with suspicions high and guns pointed at his chest, he responded that his constant thought, almost like a rosary, was simple: *I remind myself that behind that pointed gun is a human being, someone's son or daughter.*

I have heard this repeated by local peacebuilders, time and again, in very different settings. It may be the singular most surprising practice. Facing down violence requires engaging and listening to people. Listening into the depth of what brought people to violence requires the restoration of humanity.

We might call this the practice of *restorative listening.*

In another region of Colombia, the founders of the Association of Campesinos and Workers mentioned earlier, provide another example. They operationalized restorative listening in the form of a principle: *We commit ourselves to understanding those who do not understand us.*

I also heard this from Brendan McAllister[8] in Northern Ireland as we emerged from a soul-numbing meeting with an unrepentant gunman in the Maze Prison, a person who had systematically gunned down people at funeral.

During the hours of that conversation, I listened as an outsider. Brendan sat in as a person not only from the context, but from the opposing side of this gunman's identity. I asked Brendan how he did it, how he prepared day after day in his mediation work to engage people who saw his community as the enemy. His response:

I guess my practice is simple enough. No matter the person across from me, it is up to me, it is my responsibility to protect their dignity. I cannot ask of them what I am not willing to offer.

There is nothing easy about being born to generational trauma. Far too often for far too many, direct experiences of loss and harm mixed with intergenerational trauma lingers just below the surface of conversations and relationships.

There is nothing easy about sitting with deep grievance, the kind that cannot listen beyond its own pain. Arguing with grievance, offering facts and evidence, rarely proves effective. It reinforces the needs to defend and blame.

On the other hand, listening that seeks to understand those who do not understand us holds the potential to open a more reflective encounter for all participating. I suppose this has much to do with *patient ears* and an *unhurried tongue*.

Elise Boulding, one of my mentors, referred to this as *prophetic listening*: The practice of listening in such a way that the person speaking has opportunity to reflect at a new level on their search for meaning. At its essence, prophetic listening offers spaciousness. It is not driven by putting forward solutions, making demands, judging, justifying, or blaming. Prophetic listening opens the potential that the person speaking has the space to hear themselves, to listen into their own deepest understanding. This, in turn, opens the potential to move beyond defensiveness and blame.

The lives of others, their lived experiences, are never as simple as we presume. Beneath what may appear as absolute conviction, a deeper flow of hopes and loss is hidden. It takes time and care for this deeper flow to rise through the hard crust of pain.

Whether we recognize it or not, breaking through toxic polarization and violence always requires the inner works needed to witness and stay curious about the lives of other people, especially those who we find threatening.

Throughout *The Pocket Guide*, we return to the practice of curiosity. Curiously, the word curious shares a common etymology with verbs like to cure, to curate, and even to care. To be curious is to care about others' lives. Consider for moment the social impacts of the absence of curiosity, whether about others or oneself.

Incuriosity falls consistently back to cycles of self-justification and blame.

Incuriosity about how we respond to the world around us, what hooks us, what makes us defensive, blinds us to our own carried trauma.

Incuriosity about others, particularly those perceived as enemies, will consistently undermine any ability to sit with another's experience and story.

If the purpose is to shift the patterns by which grievance justifies dehumanizing violence, then the challenge of remaining curious about self and other, the challenge of entering the terrain of story and lived experience, requires the commitment to restore humanity.

It is striking that our dictionaries offer definitions of *dehumanization*, but never for *rehumanization*.

The core challenge in facing deep grievance remains how we find our way back to shared humanity in the midst of ever-unfolding harm. The commitment to shift this dynamic remains the primary starting point for many who have taken up the challenge to mitigate or reverse the landscape of violence. The practice of restorative listening helps us create a path toward this practical principle: Learn first how to sit with another's story before you shift the morals of the stories.

Morals of the stories in plural because bearing witness to another's story will always have you sitting with the perceptions, gaps, and aspirations of your own.

Curiosity is never a one-way street.

The unexpected practice that rises to challenge holy grievance emerges from commitment to curiosity carried with patience and embodied in the discipline of listening to understand.

Patient ears. Unhurried tongue.

CHAPTER 4

The Rituals of Fear

Their first worry is not about your behavior. First and last,
they focus on your fear. If they control your fear, they
control your feet.

Campesino leader, personal conversation,
Medio Magdalena, Colombia, 2005

Walking streets in contested cities offers a window into the nature
of armed pockets, the power of *performative* violence, and the ritual
of fear.

I remember an experience in Bogotá in the mid-1990s with a close
friend, Ricardo Esquivia, an Afro-Indigenous peace leader and human rights lawyer.[9] We were staying at his house, and our daily
walk to and from our meeting venue took about thirty minutes.
Each morning and evening I followed his lead. And each time we
came and went to our meeting, we took a different route.

One evening I said, "Ricardo, I am enjoying the views of these
different neighborhoods, but I am not learning how to find my
way back and forth to your house because we never take the same
street."

He paused and said something to this effect: *You are looking at the map of streets. They are visible and have names. I am watching the landscape of threats. They are invisible and have no names.*

In 2021, I had a conversation with several long-term peace activists from Belfast. They were young adults when the Troubles began and are now in their seventies and eighties.

One of them told a story about walking home from the center of Belfast just a day before our conversation. Midway on her return, she stopped on one of the streets in a moment of revelation, laughing at herself. She had taken the long route home, the way that was safe during the Troubles some two decades earlier. Now a far shorter route was possible, but, as she put it, *her habit forgot* and the rituals of precaution and fear still guided her feet. She concluded her story reflecting that *we just don't realize how deep violence penetrates.*

In settings of sustained armed conflict, especially in pockets where a dominating armed presence is sought, violence is often deployed with performative purpose.

By performative violence, I refer to way it is utilized to denigrate and degrade. Its purpose is to embody humiliation. Or, as is too often the case, to literally disembody as humiliation.

The tactical goal of performative violence is fear.

The strategic goal of performative violence is submission.

I spent the past five years in close touch with Father Francisco de Roux[10] in his role as the head of the Colombian Truth Commission.[11] The hardest moments I imagine for him personally, and certainly for me as a listener, came when he publicly recounted, almost as litany, the wretchedness of performative violence that he had witnessed and attended to in his thousands of conversations across the country: Chain sawed arms, a fetus hung on a door, a father's head used as a football.

His question was always the same: How did this happen on our watch?

In armed pockets, fear functions to assure what Colombians call *the law of silence*. I have heard this kind of phrase invoked countless times in other places. People describe what happens when armed groups arrive and in plain sight devastate families and whole communities, while always letting some live as witnesses. Their message was always the same: *You saw us. You saw what we did. You are left alive. Never use your tongue to speak our names.*

Recall in the little town of La India in Medio Magdalena, a paramilitary commander gave the community four choices when he offered them guns: *Stay and join us, you will be safe. Join them, and we are coming for you. Don't take these guns, just choose to leave and become one of the millions displaced. Or stay, don't take the guns, don't join us, and we will kill you.* His purpose was fear and submission.

How does fear become so ritualized?

The signs seem to be these. Start with open armed presence. Make a show of it. Then deploy threats until they abound. To reinforce the threat, use sporadic and targeted violence to make an example of a few. Re-deploy threats, so many that it becomes hard to know which will become actionable. Do all this publicly, especially in places where public security is too tenuous to respond in a timely manner. Spread slowly across new geographies. Do not overreach, but repeat. Never stop the repeat.

With enough repetition, people find the habits of response emerge. Some will find it easier to join than resist. There is, after all, a form of solidarity that comes with a singularity of truth and the piercing clarity of the outside enemy. For others, survival or protection of family become paramount: Leave. Avoid confrontation. Choose silence.

In the famous words of the poet Irish poet Seamus Heaney: *Whatever you say, say nothing.*[12]

For many, leaving seems the only choice available. Across our globe, feet speak more to the impact of violence than anything else. In 2023 alone, 100 million people fled from war and armed threat.

In most every setting of protracted violent conflict, I notice that the pace of performative violence has always outpaced the pace of institutional response.

The vacuum creates the space for the rituals of fear to become habit.

My friend from Northern Ireland was right. Violence penetrates deep.

My friend from Medio Magdalena was right. The performers of violence do not worry about your behavior. They focus on controlling your fear.

People in local communities facing repeated cycles of violence have much to share about fear because it forms the fabric of their daily lives.

Across very diverse settings of civil wars, I have consistently found that their starting point rarely focuses on finding the magic formula for overcoming fear.

The great surprise is how they adapt by embracing fear as a constant companion.

They do not frame their challenge as how to overcome fear. They view the challenge as learning to *walk with and through fear*, a pathway of dignity leading into purposeful action.

The *campesinos* from Medio Magdalena who formed their association known at the ATCC proposed at least three principles they followed when deciding on actions for how to face armed militias.

Their first was shown in their *internal* preparation. Remarkably similar to the Women of Wajir half a world away, they would sit and discuss what they knew. Much of their conversation focused on who they needed to reach and who among them would lead the reaching. This involved risk and was never taken lightly.

For this reason, *internal* had two meanings with two different elements of how they prepared.

Internal meant that they deliberated openly within their circle. These were often extended exchanges with full expression of differences and concerns.

Internal also meant that each of them knew they had to build their individual resolve. They had to foster the courage to reach out toward the source of their threats — the fortitude needed, as individuals and together, to step beyond the safety of their trusted circle.

The key resides in *doing it together*. Never was any action taken alone. They always worked and traveled in small groups.

Their second principle: Through the conversations, they developed clarity about specific and very concrete changes their actions would seek to achieve.

Third, they employed a strategy of *circulating*. Literally, many of their actions required a small group to travel and seek out conversation with those who had created harm in their communities.

Their commitment was such that they specifically note this as part of their original guiding principles when they formed the organization: *We have no enemies. We will negotiate with everyone.*

They rarely, if ever, *convened* dialogue meetings or peace conferences. Once they achieved clarity about who they needed to talk with, specificity on the change they hoped to engender, and who would lead the reaching out beyond their inner circle, only then would small groups deploy. They would seek out the armed groups and leaders they sought to engage. And they would circulate throughout the area where they lived.

Embedded in this strategy we find their imagination of risk: They consistently took *one small risk* at a time around *one concrete idea* with the *right people* in the lead.

Compare the ATCC approach employed in the late 1980s in Colombia with a recent conversation I had with Rose Acindhel.[13] Rose has worked for many years in communities affected by violence, communities often controlled by armed groups in her home country of South Sudan.

Rose suggests three elements for walking with and through fear: Take courage. Be resilient. Be patient.

Courage, she says, comes from working in smaller and often diverse groups. Her words: *Never work or travel alone. Courage always rises from encouragement.*

Resilience, Rose notes, is not so much about being long suffering in the Judeo-Christian scriptural wisdom translations for patience.

Resilience is not about accepting suffering as the universal standard. According to Rose, resilience describes the commitment to *keep in mind* the goals, the case you want to make to people (especially those carrying guns), and the basic hopes of the wider community to live free of violence.

Patience, she suggests, is important because you need to find the wisdom of how best to approach any given conversation and how to bring transparency to the community and the people you seek to engage. Patience as a practice for walking with fear enables you to respect the local context and create the pace of conversation and action that reduces suspicion and fosters openness.

In all these examples, we find an unexpected gift: Fear slows you down.

People in settings of violence understand the paradox of fear: Fear paralyzes. And. Fear teaches.

Collective courage will be needed to face the paralysis. This rises from careful observation. It asks you to watch your pockets, to notice and learn from people and the place where you live.

Fear teaches you to slow down enough to detect the signs of threat and possibility.

Fear demands you consider those things you must avoid and to specify the core aspirations you must find a way to achieve.

What might we draw from these people who learned to face and then *walk with and through* fear to shift toxic patterns of division and violence?

Pursue clarity of purpose. Be patient. Respect local understanding. Take time to listen together. Nurture inner conviction. Foster collective courage. Nudge the boundary of who you reach, and you will nudge the toxicity of isolation and reciprocal harm.

Act. Together. One risk at a time. Learn. Repeat.

CHAPTER 5

The 90% Rule
The inner works of isolation

When they first see you, he paused, lifted his head, and sniffed the air, *they will be taking a whiff of what air you bring, of what you're up to. They will have no time for anything that wastes their time because they do not have any time. They will know in a minute or two. Anything that smells of danger or traps will get nothing but reactions, rarely, if ever, reflection.*

Former Basque ETA member,
the Basque Country, 1995

I always found it puzzling that people can fight decades of war and have so little time to talk about how it might end, or what might constitute the foundations for talks. Or even *talks about talks.* In the exchange with our friend above just prior to our meeting with his former colleagues, he called it the 90% rule.

His experience suggested this. Living at the far margin of the rule of law while still circulating openly, focusing almost exclusively on logistical demands of the *next operation,* and keeping all communication hidden — these swallow all your time. Navigating daily, even hourly concerns contributes to having no time to think about the big picture or the wider purpose of all these endeavors. Energy focuses full-time on the next campaign.

As he conveyed it:

They spend 90% of their time in operations. Maybe they have 10% available for thinking. There is a very high chance they will have no answers to any of your questions. They do not have time for thinking about anything new. It's the ninety percent rule: Just keep the operations moving.

On a very different front, during the U.S. electoral campaign of 2004, the capacity for large-scale data analysis of partisan communication patterns achieved greater sophistication.

Blogs, Twitter, postings on Facebook, opinion pieces — all entered and circulated across the digital world as traceable data. Once available as data, researchers with increasingly sophisticated data visualization tools could trace where an idea, a conversation, or a proposal originated and then traveled. Data became artwork.

One article and the authors' visualization caught my attention.[14] Their inquiry traced data around how ideas once published in political blogs were shared: *Where did the conversations digitally travel? With whom were they shared? Where did they not travel?*

The visual artwork presented two bright bubbles in Venn diagram format. One was red, one was blue — representing political preferences in the U.S. In the graphic, the two bubbles appeared to be separating, like an amoeba about to break apart. Between the red and blue bubbles, a fragile, nearly invisible yellow set of lines indicated where the conversations had crossed from one "world" of discourse to the other. One finding stood out in Lana Adamic and Natalie Glance's explanation.

In fact, 91% of the links originating within either the conservative or liberal communities stay within that community.

These two "90% anecdotes" precisely match the dynamic I have often found in settings of protracted violent conflict and shed light on the what we could call the *challenge of isolation*: How is it possible to live side-by-side in totally different realities that produce a common experience of suffering at the hands of the "other side"?

Protracted conflicts create and rely on isolated bubbles to replicate mutual exclusion. Consider the functions that isolation produces.

Isolation serves to uphold the ideological or political purity of discourse *within* a community. We might call this "toeing the party line." Isolation serves to keep everyone very busy talking with people who already agree with each other.

At the same time, as external threats increase, isolation reduces internal dissent. This serves to narrow the space for questioning leadership. People simply cannot afford to disagree when under threat. Dissent within a group is portrayed as betrayal, as debilitating *us* and aiding the enemy. With even the slightest mention of a different point of view, suspicion abounds: *Whose side are you on?*

Throughout, the dynamics of isolation serve to minimize contact and interaction with the complexity of issues and situations present at any given moment. A singularity of understanding dominates, one that aligns with predetermined explanations and forms the narrative held within the bubble. The only facts accepted are those that align with what is already known and accepted.

Colombians describe these dynamics as the *yo-con-yo* conversation. Translated, *yo-con-yo* means, "I talk with myself." In practice, it means that I only talk with people who already agree with me.

Yo-con-yo is like the childhood toy called the yo-yo. A yo-yo is permitted to travel, but only up and down the string. The rotating yo-yo always arrives back exactly where it started.

As polarization intensifies, the frequency of conversations with those who agree with each other increases while the contact with those in disagreement decreases.

Under threat we feel a need to talk with those who *feel* our threat. We become busy talking with people who agree with us. The impact on communication is that we talk more and more *about* those who we do not like while we talk less and less *with* them.

Intense polarization and armed conflict serve to keep more extreme leadership in place.

More extremist views in leadership happen because in settings of deep conflict people fear the consequences of isolation. Worse, they fear the label of having betrayed the home community and aided the enemy.

In these settings, especially where stakes are extremely high with actual violence, it only takes the slightest perception of traitor or spy to quickly unravel even the longest-standing relationships. And the fear of losing all of one's primary relationships constantly shapes how carefully people navigate the choice to confront leadership in settings of high conflict.

Around the table in Valledupar sat the mostly unlikely set of people one could imagine in this long-conflicted Department of Cesar in Colombia. Through the afternoon and well into the evening over drinks, people from across the political, social, and cultural spectrum talked, laughed, told hard stories, got angry, accused, and defended. The descent into anger and defensiveness would normally have shattered a gathering like this. But instead of leaving, people stayed in conversation. More importantly, they stayed in relationship across their historic divides that had been at the heart of long-standing armed conflict, something so unlikely that they referred to themselves as the *Improbables*.[15]

They have been side-by-side for a while. The meetings I watched unfold were not their first. In fact, their gatherings number in the dozens. Starting off in smaller groups, at times with long one-on-one conversations, the gatherings grew to twenty or more people. Their meals and meetings were held out of the public eye. They found a way to keep coming back to talk together and over time an unexpected dynamic emerged: They found themselves moving from knowing about the other to acknowledging their humanity and learning the art of patience with their enemies.

It is said that the best way to get rid of enemies is to make them your friend. Something of that nature seemed emergent. Enmeshed with such a significant shift, we find something important: People in this group were experiencing and learning ways to *enemy better*. They still saw themselves as *opuestos*, on opposites sides of the conflict and views of history and harm. And yet they found their way to engagement through dialogue without violence.

Being better *opuestos* requires honesty and patience with deep differences even as polarization remains stark. And all this emerged in a region of Colombia renowned for high levels of violence.

How did they face down the dynamics of isolation that sustained this violence for years?

First, their process never proposed a negotiation or getting together to agree. If they had a pact, it was only on agreed ways of *being* together. Their table was for eating and drinking together.

They created a kind of social *sancocho*, this cultural culinary word for a hearty stew that typically adds whatever vegetables and meat might be available, simmers for hours, and then is served to gather and feed whole families and communities.

They called their home-grown stew the *Diálogos Improbables*, the Improbable Dialogues. To be clear, the term *improbable* doesn't mean hopeless. It means that unless there was intentionality, this group would not have come together. In other words, improbable conveys the audacity to meet. It's the antonym of *yo-con-yo*.

Toxic polarization will always reduce complexity to a binary. Us and them rules. We might even express this phrase as a poetic verb: *Us-and-theming*. What results is a form of social isolation defined by increasingly separate but impermeable identity groups.

Those most interested in sustaining this world of sharply divided bubbles will always manipulate by fear of social rejection, threat, and generalizations about outsiders. All this flames the dynamics that keep complexity and mutual understanding at bay and encourages the view that even the slightest contact with difference is dangerous and puts our survival at risk.

Mitigating toxic isolation requires reaching out and sustaining diverse and unlikely relationships. While never easy, reaching out and developing diverse relationships stitches the social fabric necessary to reduce and prevent the threat and use of violence.

The lessons from the *Improbables* suggest how it might be possible to reverse toxicity. Here a few of their steps.

First, it begins with keeping alive at least a small dose of curiosity. Widening the container of views and experiences we encounter and interact with nurtures the potential for innovation — something new and different in a setting where people feel caught in the cycles of repeating harm.

But how to navigate the boundaries of ever hardening social bubbles?

Lessons from the *Improbables* suggests that entryways will be needed between the two worlds, entryways that will require unusual relationships. In polarized settings, change will not happen by staying in isolated bubbles. While we often imagine change as connected to a proposal or the content of ideas, people who have faced violence understand that openness to any idea is only as great as the quality of the relational context within which the idea is presented, received, entertained, and explored.

If we return to the dynamics of isolation, we recall that people do not believe if they see it — they look for what they already believe to confirm what is known. To echo an old Shakespearean turn of phrase, in highly polarized systems people *listen with their eyes.*

In toxic conflict, people rarely attend to the facts, the quality of explanation, or the insight of a proposal when it comes from a perceived enemy. Perception is everything. They look first at *who* has said something, *who* proposed it. In that quick glance, they assess who this person is, the group they associate with, and thereby situate them through the lens of threat. Categorizing a person by affiliation offers the basis for interpretation, for giving meaning to what they say.

Listening with eyes eliminates the need to be curious.

To break a bubble of isolation, something surprising will be needed. Not with reference to the content of policy, but with reference to unexpected relationships. Imagine if an unlikely pair, or several pairs — each of whom as individuals has the trust of their respective community — begins to walk together and begins to propose an idea. Now our eyes cannot automatically pigeonhole what this is about because we are not certain who it comes from. We must stop and take a second look. The arrival of *improbable relationships* even on a small scale can disrupt relentless toxicity.

Here we find a small theory of surprise: Improbable relationships create the pause of curiosity. In a sense, social change in settings of toxic polarization will always be relationship-centric. Finding living examples, small pockets of unusually engaged relationships, creates a renewed vitality of understanding and potential.

Let's return to where we started this chapter and ask about our own lives.

This week did 90% of my conversations only stay within my circle of friends that I find safe and where we all agree?

Is 90% of my time devoted to conversations where my social energy is spent blaming *others* or defending *us*?

Has it reached the point where I listen with my eyes and am no longer curious about proposals or the lives of neighbors who hold differing views?

If answers to these questions are affirmative, or close to it, take note. It suggests our web of conversations and narrowed relationships support the continuation of toxic polarization.

Settings of protracted conflict instruct us that shifting the dynamics of social isolation starts with opening conversations beyond a narrow circle of friends who all agree.

For the *Improbables*, their journey did not start by jumping to the far reaches of extremism as the first step. It started closer to home. It started with one-on-one conversations with a few neighbors, but ones who were different.

Many places I have worked use a phrase to describe their early and on-going work to halt patterns of harm with the simplest of explanations: *We started with good neighborliness.*

The simplest practices for facing down a civil war?

Start with noticing if you listen with your eyes.

Open just a slightly wider set of relationships.

Let curiosity instead of quick judgement guide your conversational journeys.

Stay in relationship with people even when you disagree.

CHAPTER 6

Growth by Fractions

*We have dems, soc-dems, pop-dems, and nat-dems and
each of those have their own subgroups. And that is just the
groups on the center-left to the far left of the political
spectrum.*

Friend explaining rise of political affiliation after the
nonviolent resistance movement to Marcos,
the Philippines, 1990

My first experience supporting a high-level political negotiation
came in the East Coast of Nicaragua. Our process lasted the better
part of a decade. It taught me about something I found common
in many other settings: Constant factionalizing of armed groups.
While we might initially imagine this as weakening movements,
the more irrepressible dynamic has something to do with *propagat-
ing-as-outcome* where fragmenting becomes a generative modality to
spread and assure continuation.

Those engaged in armed conflict face the persistent challenge of
how their movements spawn a wide array of subdivisions. If one
thing remains constant across contexts of armed conflict, it would
be the dynamic of groups splintering — the phenomenon of creating growth by way of fractionalization. In my early exposure of the
1980s, at least eight separate factions emerged in the East Coast of

Nicaragua resistance. They were based in both ethnic and geographic groups of the subregion, the largest being the Miskito Indians.

Some divisions in the resistance pertained to ethnic identity, some to geography. Others related to charismatic leaders with dedicated followers. A multi-decade lens would suggest an equally significant set of divisions took place within the historic Sandinista movement that have led to its current narrowed expression.

The same was true of the ever-shifting formations and dissolutions of subclan armed coalitions in Somalia starting in the late 1980s. A common Somali proverb captures the dynamic: *I against my brother; I and my brother against our father; my father, brothers, and I against our uncle and cousins; I and my subclan against other subclans.*

In colloquial Spanish, moving between the descriptors *factions* and *fractions* often happens when people talk about the dynamics of armed groups. This odd linguistic math captures a key feature of armed conflicts: How toxic dynamics spread and grow even though movements splinter.

Politically, we imagine division as debilitation. Whole strategies are built around divide and conquer.

We overlook how growth and survival *also* happen by way of propagation: Spawning divisions produces new life. This relates to the *web* approach that has been most effectively employed for illicit purposes — an approach enhanced significantly in the digital age. Connections between people traverse very different locations. They do not operate to perpetuate hierarchical control of decisions. They function to support the flow of ideas, moving at unprecedented pace and efficiency.

The dynamic holds true enough that global violent movements, like Al Qaeda ("the base"), intentionally rely on interlinked, decentralized cells with tentative holds on territory. Success focuses more on propagating than owning.

Mainstream political analysis depends on traditional processes. Focus is placed on more visible national speeches and debates and the outcomes of electoral processes. Attention is given to the known and well-established parties. Less energy is expended on the marginal, often shifting, coalitions that circulate with less visibility and may not be an initial factor in the recognized forum of candidates. In settings of protracted conflict, winning elections rarely translates into an increased capacity to govern.

The power of circulation is rarely fully understood or appreciated. When used for illicit purposes, it has capacity to spread ideas, shape perceptions, and consolidate narrative while remaining for the most part out of sight. This seems particularly robust where significant grievance already exists.

In deep conflict, when groups divide their ideas not only survive, but seem to have new platforms for spreading. This is how even small numbers of people with the right connections and capacity to circulate ideas impact the body politic. This *tyranny of the few* teaches us to never confuse political events with what disaffection and splintering spawns in the wider landscape.

In some places, the resulting outcome is referred to as *no peace, no war*: Even after major peace agreements have been signed, aggression and division often continue in the form of sporadic armed conflict.

In 2010, on a late morning in Kailali District of Nepal, I watched more than one hundred people gather at the edge of a forest. In the course of the day, their conversation seemed to imitate the sweltering heat. The issue they were addressing had brewed for more than a decade: Who had what rights to use this forest?

The gathering came just a few years after the declared end of the civil war. Wars never lay to rest easy.

During the war, many rural communities found themselves over-run by the armed conflict and everything armed conflict brings. Guns were more widely available. Communities suffered displace-ment. The daily struggle to find food and the materials needed to cook became ever more challenging.

For those gathered that morning, the issues that animated their conversation involved all these concerns, from displaced popula-tions to sporadic but regular violence to nonexistent local or national governance. Another key area of discussion was the pres-ence of the Mukta Kamaiya, former slaves accused of encroachment by a much larger local forest user group. An earlier national decree had released the Mukta Kamaiya from bonded labor. Without any land of their own, they had located near this forest to survive. The forest user group, however, rejected their presence, seeking to pro-tect their land and scarce resources.

People came and went, some milled about listening, and many were seated in what appeared as distinct groups. Leading the con-versation was a *spider group*. That was the name given to a small set of people, in this case seven, who had had worked for almost two years to bring these groups together. Curiously, each member of the spider group was also a member of one of the groups in conflict.

Their surprising practice: At the center of a long-standing com-munity conflict, seven people created dialogue between these stakeholders without reliance on an outside facilitator.

Spider may seem an odd term to describe a group that facilitates community dialogue. The name emerged because the facilitators had studied how spiders cover space and make webs. Their interest was in how the spider moved in space and how that movement helped them think about ways they could address fierce and often violent conflicts.

Another surprise: Their efforts did not represent the work of an impartial, outside facilitator. Those in the spider group had lived through and were still in the middle of the very conflict they were working to change.

They had to learn not only about the landscape of the conflict, but also how they might serve as a resource to transform it. Part of that meant they had to learn how to keep the trust of their own identity group while finding the courage to develop relationships on other sides of social divides. Once formed as a small group, they traveled together to visit all the affected communities. In essence, they learned to move like the spider, laying the first threads of a conversational web.

In the year and a half preceding this larger gathering, the spider group had traveled to spend time with each community affected by this forest conflict. They followed a common procedure. As the spider group had at least one member from each community, that person opened the meeting and helped the community express their experience and concerns. This happened across all the groups. Once a first round of conversations was complete, they returned numerous times to each group, sharing what had been learned and deepening the conversation. The circulating continued until a common understanding emerged across all the stakeholder groups on collectively agreed next steps. In their case, this was to hold several days of conversation together. This is what I watched evolve on a hillside at the edge of a forest in Nepal's Terai region.

Their learning process is now an organization, the Natural Resource Conflict Transformation Center-Nepal (NRCTC).[16] Their motto, translated in English: *Better relationship for sustainable peace.* Over the last decade they have helped transform and resolve hundreds of festering natural resource conflicts over land, forest, and water. They now have thousands of collaborators forming local spider groups.

The unexpected approach of NRCTC offers a way to face down the edge of violence that might be captured in a few key commitments and practices.

No conflict ever boils down to just two groups. Finding how to understand the wide diversity of people and groups within a local space requires mobilizing existing relationships in unusual ways.

Learn to work together with a few *across divides*, and the *few* can help the *whole heal.*

If you are going to travel, travel into the heart of conflict, not away from it. Travel to the locations where people live. See and feel the world from their homes and their porches.

Start small. Start local. Circulate with unusual friends. Propagate better conversations.

CHAPTER 7

It Only Takes One
How the spectacular enhances
the gravity of toxic polarization

To be honest, we are all waiting for the event. In the past,
every time a positive process aimed at ending the Troubles
initiated and got a wee bit of momentum, some group
would blow it up with a bomb. It only takes one. One event
can destroy the whole thing.

Conversation with long-time peace activist on
whether the Good Friday Agreement would last,
Northern Ireland, 1995

There is a paradoxical stasis to violence once it starts.

The center of gravity of most armed conflict is more armed
conflict.

The challenge for peace is rarely how to start the climb toward ending violence. The challenge is always how to sustain the long climb
out of violence once the first steps for peace begin, facing the reality that almost any spectacular violent event will pull the system
back to the conflict's center of gravity.

Splinter rebel groups use the spectacular just as do powerful governments. The importance of spectacle does not depend on who uses it.

The sought-after outcome? In armed conflict, it is always reciprocated violence. The spectacular deploys the *impossible to ignore* as the method to seek that reciprocation.

As mentioned in the opening citation, in Northern Ireland, people always feared that one bomb could set back years of work to end the violence. While January 6 may be seen as an extreme anomaly in the United States, the storming of parliaments has been employed from Madrid to Managua, all with an eye that it would catalyze something spectacular.

Across settings of violent conflict, belief in the power of the spectacular — this notion of it "only takes one" — remains a focus of intense interest among armed groups seeking to spark wider conflict, induce crackdowns, sidetrack peace processes, and recruit. It is also deployed on a regular basis by authoritarian leaders bent on creating fear of reprisal as the way to sustain submission.

The genius in the spectacular is its simplicity. It just takes one.

While acts of performative, spectacular violence seek to humiliate, dehumanize, and trigger a reciprocal response, we also find the spectacular employed as a surprising way of shifting toward respect and hope for a shared future. This form of the unexpected is less visible, perhaps harder to see because these expressions of the spectacular are shaped by humility and a shift away from being driven by daily crises.

When this counterintuitive approach gains visibility, it is often at those times when top leaders exemplify something different that touched the wider public imagination. Take Nelson Mandela for example.

As president, after having endured nearly three decades of prison, Mandela offered a view of what might be called the *horizon of reconciliation*. In his case, he carried forward into his presidency what he had stated in his inaugural speech: The idea that South Africa needed to find ways to be a *nation at peace with itself*.[17]

His engagement of rugby offered a highly visible spectacular event, now the stuff of literature and movies. The first Black president, Mandela proposed to embrace a national sport that was seen as white-dominated and, for many, replete with apartheid symbolism.

He did so with phrases like *one team, one nation*, which shocked the system of separation on all sides. The images of his presence at the Rugby World Cup finals were coupled with his open statements to his primary political support community, who justifiably resented the historic symbolism of the sport: *I ask you to stand by these our boys because they are our kind*.[18] He offered these spectacular words in public messages. And then he embodied and acted on those words.

Less well-known are thousands of acts within local communities of a similar ethos and courage. Take, for example, the case of a war that never happened.

Situated in West Africa, Ghana sits in a region where neighboring countries endured deep and difficult civil wars — Sierra Leone and Liberia, to mention two.

In the 1990s, Ghana faced rising internal conflicts, particularly in their Northern region, with undertones of tribal and religious differences. These community episodes of fighting could easily have escalated from sporadic into full-blown civil war.

One dispute was between two tribes with significant identity differences. The Konkombas, mostly Christian, did not have a form of high chieftaincy. The Dagombas, mostly Muslim, not only had a high chief, but tended to employ this tradition as a status of superiority. Local clashes between the two groups were becoming increasingly violent and frequent.

Intermediaries involved in mitigating the violence between the tribes describe an encounter when people from both sides had gathered to dialogue. The exchange became very difficult when the high chief of the Dagombas started by insulting the Konkombas.

Addressing himself only to the intermediaries, he began by saying that he, as the high chief, had no one to negotiate with – he would not lower himself to talk with *these young boys that had just come from the fields*. At that moment, many who were present thought this insult would unleash a war.

Surprisingly, the much younger spokesperson for the Konkomba started with a very different tone and response: *You are right my father, and I call you father because I do not wish to disrespect you.* He went on. *If we have no chief, and yet we have suffered greatly, what is left for us to do? If no one will speak with us, do we have no other pathway than violence to be heard?*

Attendees reported the subsequent silence lasted forever. The tone of voice from the young Konkomba man, the respect in his posture, and the care he took with his words rang with such authenticity. When he spoke, the chief's attitude and language shifted.

Though I insulted your people, you still called me father. It is you who speaks wisdom. We have not understood your denigration. I beg you, my son, to forgive me.

People say it was a turning point. Maybe it was the moment the start of a civil war was avoided.

The least watched war is the one that never happens. It is not news. It sits invisible in our world of public care and noticing.

The reasons for a war that never happens are many. But one clear element, perhaps the motherlode vein, may well be that a thousand unnoticed micro-spectacular acts of dignity and humility can shift toxicity enough that the knife-edge of violence is avoided.

Behind these acts, we also find a key shift in mindset about timeframes — a significant, but also less visible aspect embedded in the spectacular that is aimed to shift toxicity. Across settings of protracted conflict, a prevalent mindset about time is often expressed in some form of this simple phrase:

Once this crisis is over, we will get back to the real work.

People feel caught in the relentless cycle of crises. Expressed equally by local community activists and by national political leaders, the phrase reveals one of the great paradoxes of seeking change. It also offers a distorted reading of reality many people live by.

Why distorted? Because toxic polarization always generates *permanently emerging crises*.

Shifting toxicity in settings of violence does not hinge on suddenly getting to *the other side* of a crisis. There is no other side. We need to learn how to live creatively within the tensions of permanent crisis.

To avoid the resulting dynamics of feeling paralyzed or jumping from one crisis to the next, a mindset shift is required.

58

The shift I experienced with creative changemakers facing down armed violence embodies what we could call strategic hope.

We more often hear from analysts, policymakers, and funders that hope is not a strategy — yet another distortion.

I have never seen change in the patterns of repeated violence emerge and cohere without hope.

The challenge is how to achieve the Mandela effect that shifts the habits of paralysis or crisis-jumping: How to become long-term strategic and short-term creative. This requires a clear-eyed vision of the change desired in the future that informs the unexpected proactive response in the moment.

Violent conflict will continuously disrupt daily life. The best local practitioners of social change who faced down violence were geniuses at finding possibility even in the worst of crises.

This captures the Mandela practice, the same one embodied by the young Konkomba man.

This is how hope becomes strategic.

It is spectacular.

CHAPTER 8

The Mapping of
Where There Be Dragons

The Commission established that in the extrajudicial
executions an entramado, an overlapping framework of
state and nonstate actors, was consolidated.

Commissioner Alejandro Valencia on the
political murders in Bogotá and Soacha,
Truth Commission, Colombia, 2022

Armed conflict creates a strange cartography of relationships between politics and violence.

It's a strange map because over time it is never fully clear where one begins and the other ends.

The complexities and rapidly adapting nature of politics and violence constitute one of the reasons why negotiations to end conflict are hard to start, much less successfully implement. Oft referred to as the "negotiation table," these processes always traverse the fragility of representation. While everyday people most affected by the violence hope for an end to their turmoil, they also watch negotiations unfold with suspicion and deep questions: Who really represents who? And how do we understand and visualize the nature of their relationships?

Any map that seeks to track the connections of relationships in armed conflict will need to find ways to describe what is hidden. Two metaphors are commonly used to describe the experience of what is not fully seen: Swamps and seas.

In armed conflict, *swamp* often refers to the nebulous relationships between political and armed leaders. The term is likely used because the metaphoric bog covers up whatever has passed through, leaving no visible signs of paths or crossroads.

The second term is the expansive metaphor of the *sea*. The image references the way civil society, public institutions, state security forces, politicians, armed movements, and at times organized crime coexist in an *ebb and flow* of relationships. Sea also captures the experience of cycles of open violence, often described as coming in *waves*.

The recent example of the Colombian Truth Commission attempted to map and name the challenge of fifty years of harmful conflict. Among their biggest challenges was how best to attend to the experiences of those who suffered the violence — what they referred to as a "victim-centered approach" — while carefully exploring how and why this violence repeated itself over decades. How to name what is not fully seen or understood behind this ebb and flow? They did so through many forms of participation, from extensive interviews to the establishment of *houses of truth*, locally accessible places for people to share their lived experiences from where they resided.

In the end, the Commission rendered an extensive public report including an extraordinary transparent sharing of their processes and findings. It is never easy nor possible to fully attend to the breadth and depth of harms experienced over more than fifty years of organized armed violence that, as they note, is still ongoing.

Pursuing the questions of how and why violence repeats, commissioners often used the word *entramado* to describe the dynamics behind the resilience of harm, a term well worth unpacking.

In literature and social sciences, *entramado* may refer to an overlapping but guiding framework of analysis.

At a construction site, this term describes the crisscrossing materials of wood, metal, and cement, all latticed together to build a strong wall.

In perhaps its most common use, *entramado* has always been used to describe the weaving arts, the process by which threads and reeds intertwine into cloth, textiles, and baskets.

We also find embedded in its etymology an additional understanding of *entramado*. It has to do with the way a mix of hidden motivations and actions weave together for illicit or harmful outcomes. Some descriptions of its root suggest *entramado* seeks to *provide or prepare with cunning or cheating a tangled mess, a fraud, or a betrayal.* This hidden mix seems very proximate to the image of swamp. The toxic outcomes repeatedly emerging like waves in an endless sea.

Describing these more hidden elements between politics and violence helps explain why facing down a civil war is so challenging. It suggests the need to more fully understand the significance of why swamps and seas are such prevalent descriptors across settings of armed conflict.

Swamp is often used as a political metaphor for corruption. A cartographer might seize upon another quality: Social swamps describe conditions that make it *impossible* to trace connections and relationships. This may also explain why the prefix *para* appears so prominently in armed conflicts and civil wars.

Two usages stand out: Paramilitary and para-political. As a prefix, *para* indicates that something resembles or leads to something else. In the context of armed conflict, *para* points toward militarized and political behavior that sits at the margin of, if not outside, the rule of law.

Like a messy swamp, *entramado* describes efforts to achieve political goals and economic benefits by way of relationships that are not visible, traceable, or accountable.

For the Truth Commission, this quality defined the mix of armed groups, illicit economies, violence, and the contested edge of political life. Over time, the swamp became so normalized that it was almost impossible to make these relationships visible.

Seas, on the other hand, offer an image of constant movement, swells and waves, and also the primary location *where there be dragons* was used by sailors and mapmakers.

In many places of armed conflict, we frequently hear the phrase *waves of violence*. Invoking a sea-centered lens, this descriptor captures the experience of violence as repeatedly rising across decades and the feeling of unpredictability on a near daily basis.

Waves are curious phenomena. At some point a wave will rise and crash, its power and impact acutely felt. At the same time, waves swell back, making it hard to fully understand where any one wave ends or begins. Seas and waves have a quality of constant in-betweenness.

In most armed conflicts, the nexus of violence and politics functions much like the interaction of waves as the paramilitary and para-political begin to mix. Two qualities of this interaction stand out.

The first quality is the ability to have crisscrossing relationships between politics and violence without leaving any trace or tracks to follow that show the relationship exists.

The second is the capacity to effect harm, but in the manner of a sea swell that cannot easily distinguish between cause and outcome, flowing in continuous repetition.

The relationship of these two form what might best be described by the phrase *where there be dragons*.

In its original use, *where there be dragons* was placed on an unfinished map to mark where the known traversed into the vastness of the unknown.

This describes the lived experience in armed conflict across decades of turbulent seas: Waves of violence are continuous. Yet, no two waves are ever the same. And mucky swamps swallow the evidence of who and what produced the harm.

When the book was placed in my hands, my eyes were immediately drawn to the photo of the ceiba tree on the cover.[19]

Ceiba trees in Colombia have an interesting mix with historic transitions. A decade prior to the civil war in the United States, Colombia abolished slavery. May 21, 1851. As commemoration, President José Hilario López mandated that ceiba trees be planted across the country. Like the tree in the photo on the book cover, the ceiba rises to extraordinary heights with an extensive canopy. They can live more than 200 years.

Looking closer at the book cover, I saw that a rope was strung like a clothesline tied between trees. It held a different kind of laundry: Large posters of everyday people who were killed or disappeared in

64

the decades of violence in the region. The long line of photos waving in the wind under the ceiba formed an outdoor museum, the fruit of a participatory effort in Alta Montaña, in the region of Montes de María, Colombia. The author gifting me the book described their effort as *historical memory*.

As part of a reparations process, from 2014 to 2016, mostly youth photographers and interviewers traveled this rural region, one of the hardest-hit by waves of violence. They recorded and preserved stories, took photos of specific places and events, and documented the violence that had been suffered. Here we find an understanding of *historical memory-as-action*: The surprising practice of participatory and concurrent transparency.

In a different corner of Montes de María, another extraordinary example of this practice comes from the *Tejadoras de Mampuján*, the Women Weavers of Dreams and Flavors of Peace.[20] In March of 2000 their home community was the site of a dozen deaths and the displacement of 300 families. In the years that followed, the women began to gather, often sharing meals and quilting the story of their experience.

As Afro-Colombian founder Juana Alicia Ruiz[21] put it, sewing tapestries in which they stitched the figures of people who were lost that day was a way to remember, heal, and create a future. *To sit and talk*, she says, and quilt the history from *slavery to armed conflict*, was a way to both narrate what happened and rebuild a sense of belonging. They now have a museum that holds the tapestries and quilts with the story of their people and community.

The Women Weavers of Mampuján crafted a way to *remember forward*.

Over the last decades, countries that have traversed civil wars and armed conflict have established Truth Commissions as a nationally mandated process, typically as part of a peace agreement. These bodies often focus on verifying information and making public what has transpired. Sometimes they have narrow mandates. Sometimes they are asked to provide recommendations. They usually take a significant investment and an extended period of time to cover the long histories of the conflicts. Yet, these processes rarely can capture or attend to depth of loss and human suffering they investigate. Civil wars always breach the terrain of the unspeakable.

The deeper social significance of a truth commission is not just to establish facts or knowledge. For the many who have suffered, the core work of a commission is to create the long bridge between *knowing* and *acknowledging*, and ultimately, between *acknowledging* and *feeling acknowledged*.

In deep conflict, people know that suffering and harm are extensive. But this knowing too often remains in the vacuum of public silence. The bridge from knowing to acknowledging starts by moving from silence to public naming, from invisiblization to collective validation. This creates the conditions for victims to feel seen and acknowledged. In some cases, this can lead to meaningful repair and steps toward healing.

The question remains: How do whole communities, how does a whole-body politic, practice such social transparency in the context of actions hidden in the mix of violence and politics?

Journalism is an evident and significant avenue. Day-to-day it tends to capture what is *known now* of immediate events. We often hear journalists say "our reporting suggests," indicating that only small pieces of a puzzle have been explored. With time, some forms of journalism can investigate and render fuller reports. In the everyday, however, journalism tends to respond to the demands of fast-changing public attention, what is commonly called "news cycles."

In Montes de María, the book in my hand captured the outcome of a process that developed a different approach: How local communities can participate together in exploring the hidden suffering in their own backyards. We might refer to this as *participatory transparency*. It is also a very different way to address the swamps and seas close to home.

Community-based, participatory memory requires conversation about what transpired in the past in a particular location. At the same time, the creation of a collective process of searching together for meaning about this difficult past contributes to belonging and a shared future. In a sense, the practices of participatory transparency relate to the very nature of what it means to be human, together.

Nobel laureate and neuroscientist Gerald Edelman noted that we humans handle and makes sense of time in our *remembered present*.[22] That was an evocative title he gave one of his books. In his words, "every act of perception is to some degree an act of creation, and every act of memory is to some degree an act of imagination."

Community-based story gathering while people are still living in the throes of violence offers a pathway for shifting from passive knowing into acknowledging, from waiting into agency. It can bring back a sense of purpose and aliveness to what violence has sought to deaden.

The processes described suggest that bringing greater transparency to the mix of politics and violence requires community and place-based gathering of lived experience. From the efforts to document the legacy through photos and interviews, to the ways that women quilted their shared stories, they embody memory and connection.

What lessons might we gain from these recent examples in Colombia that address the dynamics of swamps and seas?

In these exemplars we find people who together opened toward and shed light on their lived experience in ways that both addressed the past and wove community.

Participatory transparency, finding ways to create shared houses of truth, does not focus on a narrow view of legal facts. It opens a process of mutual respect, of moving from knowing to acknowledging — a significant way to move through and beyond the long patterns of repeated violence. This kind of transparency, in many regards, is the opposite dynamic of a swamp that hides its relationships and behavior. Instead, it jointly builds shared spaces of recognition, mutual accountability, and belonging — creating a shared map where once there be dragons.

Social healing will always require remembering forward.

Together.

In the places where we live.

And it never has to wait for the crisis to be over before the steps to story together begin.

CHAPTER 9

Leading from the Wake

The day he agrees to give up one gun is the day he'll get a bullet in the back of his skull. And it won't come from the other side.

Conversation with an IRA man about one of
his political leaders in the push of final negotiations,
Northern Ireland, 1998

Armed conflict spawns an odd and powerful symbiosis of leadership.

Odd because with time, it becomes difficult to distinguish who leads and who follows.

Violence is always symbiotic: As leaders who pronounce and followers who act spiral amid rising toxic polarization, each nourishes the other until they can no longer survive without each other.

Symbiosis in plant life typically refers to positive mutual benefit. Public leaders openly provoke dehumanization and emphasize threat to survival. The toxicity induces a negatively spiraling dependency with their followers. In my experience, at some this point, this dependency will spawn resentment.

In settings of armed conflict, a common pattern emerges as public leaders denounce the threat from the other side and appeal for the need to respond with equal force. When followers respond with armed action — either with carefully coordinated preparation or spontaneously from rage — the public figures then back away from responsibility for the action taken, leaving their followers feeling betrayed. The violent reaction catalyzes yet another counteraction from the other side of public denouncement and demands. Once caught in this spiral, leaders at some point find that what they have birthed grows offshoots they no longer fully control.

In essence, leadership finds itself *leading from the wake* of these mutually dependent behaviors.

In settings of open violence, public leaders need but fear their own followers. Followers need but often resent their leaders. The safest place for both to land only drives the toxicity further: Create internal cohesion by increasing the sense of external, imminent threat to survival.

External threat functions like a balm for inner divisions. Felt threat catalyzes ever more extreme rhetoric in response. It justifies what is perceived and portrayed as defensive violence. Receiving violent backlash from the other side is the very thing needed to confirm that the threat is real.

Paradoxically, one of the core functions of conflict can be its binding effects, notably how internal cohesion increases with outside threat. Less noticed from a systemic view: Enemies are bound together, particularly leaders who base their popularity on more extreme views. They need the mutuality of response to generate the continued spiral of conflict.

Lest we miss the key point, toxic polarization and armed conflict serve to *paralyze* the very heart of politics, the pursuit of collective decision-making for a wider common good. War is not politics by other means. It is the destruction of reasoned exchange by way of fear, threat, and death, the ultimate form of exclusion.

In armed conflict, I have learned to *pay less attention* to the extremity of public accusatory rhetoric and to *pay more attention* to the actions of what some call the "first followers." Evidence and lived experience suggest that while the public leader's pronouncements create an opening, the first followers' actions generate momentum that forges social safety for others to join.

Finally, we find one repeating paradox about leading from the wake: Top political and public leaders in settings of armed conflict are *perceived* as incredibly powerful, but they *feel* powerless, often leading to an intense need to control. The pursuit of that control soon becomes all consuming.

In high conflict, public leadership becomes less about producing good or even winning, and far more about maintaining domination both within their own movements and across social and political divides.

Among the most startling of dynamics experienced by leaders in highly polarized and openly violent settings is an overwhelming, though rarely confessed, sensation of abject loneliness. Isolation, fear, and loneliness tend to beget paranoia and extreme control, which in turn fuel the negative symbiosis of dependency and resentment.

Leading from the wake suggests that a key to facing down a civil war requires finding a way to step away from the known cycles of repeated violence and into the unknown arena of redefining relationships such that politics without violence becomes the norm. Stepping into the unknown, however, will always require living as a leader with less control. Therein we find the deep challenge of shifting the tides of violence: How to move from obsession for control toward *engaged openness.*

Ballu Chaudhary's question left a palpable silence in the room.

We were in the agricultural training center in Bhaktapur, Nepal. It was the early process of developing approaches to a wide array of natural resource conflicts with leaders of what would become the National Resource Conflict Transformation Center. We were working with the forest and water user groups experiencing increasing levels of local violence over these disputes at the same time as they traversed the legacies of the national civil war.

Balluji came from the Mukta Kamaiya community. When he was 18 years old, his extended family gained freedom from bonded slavery. His personal life changed forever as he lived through the challenge of where his people, with nothing but the clothes on their backs, would find a place to live and survive.

As a younger member of his group who spoke multiple languages, Balluji was often called upon to meet with people who viewed his community as encroachers when they set up temporary homes at the edge of forests and close to rivers. While meeting these challenges, he pursued and formed relationships with members of a local forest user group, a collective perceived as enemies by his community. Balluji's unusual connections placed him at the center of these natural resource conflicts.

Living between conflicting groups, being pulled in two directions, is never easy. The natural fruit of toxic polarization is not only the rise of more strident leadership. It also places pressure on people with relationships on both sides to declare their loyalty.

For Balluji, his moving back and forth between groups feeling this pressure to choose between them troubled him deeply. In our meeting of spider group members, he shared his frustration.

I am lost – not sure what I should do. When I meet with my family and the Kamaiya leaders, they tell me, Balluji, you are one of us. You must represent us. You must defend us against them. But when I meet with my friends in the forest user group, they say the same thing: You are one of us. You must defend us against the Kamaiya demands. Traveling with the spider group, now I am not sure. Who am I? Am I with the Kamaiya? Am I with the forest user group? Or am I just a nobody?

The silence that followed his question was revealing. There was not a person in the room who did not experience the same tension. From that point forward, we referred to this as Balluji's Dilemma.

In high conflict, the fault lines of identity demand complete loyalty, forcing strict adherence to the exclusionary binary of *us versus them*. Intensifying polarization serves not only to divide, but to divide with unfiltered animosity – the desire to dominate the other driven by socially reinforced fear of being dominated by the other.

Described less frequently is the lived experience of people who have significant relationships on both sides, even though this remains the unspoken reality for many people in settings of conflict.

Sometimes we capture this dynamic with the terminology of the "quiet middle," or the "silent majority." Such terms do not fully capture the experience. It can be paralyzing, this ongoing and intensifying demand to define oneself in favor of one group or the other. The struggle does not center on the search for right and wrong. The deeper internal wrestling is about the wrenching experience of breaking and losing significant family and friendships.

This was the gist of Balluji's Dilemma: How do I lead when my relational fabric is fraying?

The unexpected practice this wider movement found as they responded to volatile natural resource conflicts was that *quality of their presence* mattered more than having a perfect solution or controlling people or process. What made a difference was what people experienced and felt through the movement members' commitment to be alongside, listen, and encourage.

Leaders embedded in settings of deep conflict who shift the dynamics of toxicity do not perfect the art of unflawed speech or how to craft the ideal proposal. Rather, they hone a way of connecting authentically to lived experience that permits the courage to engage difference while opening a pathway to redefining relationships and reducing reactivity. At essence, their presence embodies respect.

None of the qualities that define this presence are passive, middle of the road, or diluted to avoid difference or win victories. Those involved in the spider groups helped shape a presence that shifted the social dynamics from avoidance to engagement, from reaction to interaction, from defensiveness to openness, from blame to proposal.

Quality of presence may seem an odd descriptor, but the landscape of toxic polarization is always defined more by feeling than fact. To the point: When we sense reactivity aimed our way, we feel anxious and drawn to protect ourselves. We often react more forcefully as a measure of self-preservation. When we experience blame, we feel judged. When we feel judged, we become defensive.

When we experience these dynamics in combination — arrogance, reactivity, blame, judging, and defensiveness — particularly when posed as superiority, we feel belittled. We shut down. We move away. We defend. We protect. Or we react with greater counter-force.

In all instances, we retreat to safety. Our primary group becomes the safe house. And the world out there, populated with those who are different, becomes the danger zone.

Learning to embrace Balluji's Dilemma suggests another pathway: How to stay true to personal conviction while creating leadership that respects difference and opens toward collective understanding and action.

What lessons might we draw for how to face down the dynamics of leading from the wake and the toxicity it depends on and then reproduces?

Remember that while most of us are *followers*, with a bit of courage, we will discover we can *lead* into *humanizing* the conflict wherever we live.

Give less energy to worrying about the strident leader.

Focus more on people who can sustain friendships across divides despite the social pressure. Together find ways to build this unusual presence amid the toxicity that resists the shredding of relationships and holds a wider social fabric together.

Try practicing and offering three gifts.

The gift of clarity: When facing tensions of deep difference, share your best understanding of your views and proposals without judgment or retreat.

The gift of curiosity: Interact with others' experiences and ideas rather than reacting quickly or judging, particularly when you feel confronted.

The gift of perseverance: Find ways to stay in touch. Keep circling back. After all, humanizing always needs a human touch.

CHAPTER 10

Drawing Lines
The long search for belonging

gods and men love maps
they draw borders with pens that
split lives like an ax

Settings of civil wars that rise from or contribute to the delineation of boundaries for predetermined outcomes always end up with a pen drawing oddly shaped borders that split lives and sow the seeds of disenfranchisement.

The haiku above was written in Dushanbe in the early 2000s. Tajikistan was on the other side of a civil war. I was working with thirty professors from seven universities to develop a curriculum on conflict, peace, and the contributions of the Tajik experience.

We traveled extensively in the Fergana Valley. I recall how my Tajik colleagues talked about their history, poets, cultural heritage, and borders. They often pointed out the legacy of those lines on a map, the ones arbitrarily dividing countries. The haiku conveys part of saying in Tajik, the bit about how pens act as an ax.

Border-drawing pens were fluid in this valley where Tajiks, Uzbeks, and Kyrgyz share and contest their lands and heritages. Borders did not follow geographic contours nor the distribution of ethnic identities. In fact, the opposite held: Borders were reduced to administrative decisions under Joseph Stalin in the 1920s focused on making transportation fluid for Soviet economic benefit and mitigating potential ethno-religious resistance within countries of the Union.

The strategy seemed to follow at least one key authoritarian principle: To exert uncontested political control, spread your minorities. Bend the pen to keep those you fear split.

Not all civil wars generate new maps. But many have and many will.

Civil wars have never solved for the deeper problem behind the map drawing — the long search for place, dignity, and belonging.

Too many wars are fought over who holds the pen and whose lives will be split by the ax.

Assumptions abound that if borders are better drawn, narrowed, or expanded to solidify primary identities, peace will ensue.

With long histories and recently explosive armed conflicts, stark examples suggest the opposite holds true: Ethiopia, Eritrea, and Tigray. Sudan and South Sudan.

Every new line drawn still leaves untouched the deeper challenge of belonging: How to assure respect for dignity, security, and the place of difference, particularly for minorities held within majority populated boundaries.

The aspiration to assure belonging suggests that humanity cannot escape the nature of our *ultimate interdependence*. No matter the number of civil wars pursued in the name of more differentiated *independence*, the need for recognition, respect, and dignified belonging amidst diversity remains present and, as history shows, powerful in how it manifests.

How best to cultivate belonging amidst diversity poses this challenge across settings of civil wars: When interdependence transfigures to exclusionary formulas based on control or choosing between us or them, violence often emerges in response as the ultimate choice in the search for survival.

Comparative data exploring the implementation of peace accords attempting to end civil wars demonstrate the challenge. In the thirty-five major agreements seeking to end civil wars since the late 1980s, minority rights rarely appear. Where these rights were included, their implementation remains among the least fulfilled stipulation.

Around the Fergana Valley, rich in resources, Stalin set his sights on creating the conditions for permanent control. He accomplished this in part by solidifying a negative stasis of identity separation and divisions of local power: Give identity groups some, but not full, internal control in each country, keeping some of their group as minorities within the others.

In the 1920s Stalin's pen was powerful. And adaptive. His ax was sharp. When the wars eventually erupted sixty years later, they were "civil wars," mostly exploding from within the boundaries he had drawn.

The impulses behind gerrymandering in the United States seem driven by these same impulses of political control rarely built on the aspirations of dignified belonging.

If our inquiry seeks to understand how best to prevent the rise of violence, the lessons of civil wars suggest we pay closer attention to the power of pens and axes that affront dignity. Boundary drawing to divide communities may offer short-term political control, but they cultivate the soils of long-term resentment.

In every preceding chapter the strategies for facing down armed conflict described the inverse of what penholders of division fail to understand. Relationships of dignity and dialogue amidst diversity are the pillars that sustain the social contract of politics without violence.

Politics wielding the pens that split lives like an ax only increase the longer-term potential that a house divided will not stand.

Conclusions

The preceding chapters outline various patterns and dynamics I have experienced as prevalent in settings where toxic polarization and open violence mix and dominate the life and landscape of politics.

In those settings, older generations often recall a time before their country was overtaken by cycles of armed conflict. They mention that they knew deep challenges and divisions existed, but never imagined they could translate to such levels of hostility, open violence, and suffering. They struggle to identify an exact moment when sporadic but organized violence found the soil to root and propagate, becoming sustained. References are given to spectacular events, often qualified with lament about the accumulating deterioration of the basic social fabric.

People that have faced open armed conflict consistently recall that they did not believe that the unraveling into sustained violence would end up dominating their lives and political landscape. At the same time, violence was not equally distributed. More common was that some regions suffered more direct violence than others, particularly along rural and urban divides.

The Pocket Guide posed a framing question: How can everyday people face down a system of toxic polarization leading into violence?

Summarizing across the chapters, three prominent themes stand out.

PATTERN 1
Toxicity Proliferates

The most significant pattern remains the capacity of social and political dynamics to reproduce collective harm over time.

Toxicity lives to replicate itself.

Extreme toxicity always unfolds with serrated edges of open violence.

First assumed as an outlier, that violence increasingly becomes the defining norm.

Once unleashed, armed conflict becomes very difficult to stop and creates unspeakable harm.

People who have lived with civil war learn to watch these edges where toxicity and violence converge. They particularly recognize the deteriorating quality of relationships precisely because toxic polarization seeks to fray the social fabric.

PATTERN 2
Dehumanization Dominates

For toxic polarization to reproduce itself, it must feed and be fed by dehumanizing dynamics.

Differentiation — us and them — is a natural part of a dynamic, creative, social, and political life. Polarization *per se* is not the problem. Rather, it is dehumanization, which, when intensified in a reactive system, escalates polarization from healthy to poisonous.

Dehumanization denies the humanity of those deemed other.

Stated slightly differently, dehumanization invisibilizes the humanity of the other — their existence, their life, their story — and enwraps itself in an overwhelming sense of threat to survival that justifies the suffering of others to protect ourselves.

Dehumanization sharpens the intensity of our pain because it expresses itself with piercing humiliation. A common outcome: We become oblivious and numb to the suffering of those we perceive as different, threatening, or as the cause of our pain.

Those who have faced the dynamics of a civil war have lived experience in how social numbness grows. When we no longer are capable of noticing and feeling the suffering of others, a compassion deficit becomes deep and prevalent within our torn social fabric.

PATTERN 3
Paralysis Propagates

Paralysis of leadership at all levels forms a third consistent pattern and outcome of toxic polarization. It is one of the experiences most shared across settings of civil wars. People feel stuck.

Paralysis appears time and again by blaming others and believing that nothing can be done. Even thinking about alternatives is derided as a fool's errand. This tends to normalize a kind of social and political realism bereft of imagination.

Settings of armed conflict teach us just how much paralysis propagates.

At local levels, an attitude can prevail where we presume that we must wait for another level of authority to act. Suffering and frustration can easily express themselves through blame, grievance, and, ultimately, dependency. This explains the most common feeling experienced at grassroot levels about elite peace processes: National politics is too distant. They do not see us.

At higher political levels, the permanently emerging crises create a continuous flow of calamities, each replete with dysfunctional dynamics and each a seed to replicate the next. Repeat and replicate. The greatest contribution of a new crisis is the doorway it opens to deflect, denounce, and justify.

Toxic polarization fosters the perception that any proposal for change is dead before it has even been spoken. It's an odd logic that creates and sustains the norm that the only thing *they* understand is the very thing *we* would never accept.

The good news is that people have imagination and capacity to respond in surprising ways to shift these patterns of toxicity. What do we make of everyday people who, through their positive deviance, shifted away from toxicity and violence while it was still raging? From my experience, three core insights seem to crisscross and underpin the practices of the unexpected that gave rise to constructive change.

INSIGHT 1
Humanize the Face of Conflict

In settings of sustained violence, there are no shortcuts. It requires sustained resistance to patterns of dehumanization. The search for respect involves the offer of dignity — the recognition that every person has inherent undeniable worth.

For local communities, innovations that shift toxicity embody imagination and the moral capacity to enact immediate response

84

to crisis challenges in service of a longer-term shared future. This clarity of horizon, remembering forward, understands that victory in the form of humiliating defeat is not the guiding star. Horizon clarity is about healing.

Seamus Heaney described healing as having this beacon quality, a distant shore that can be reached.[23]

Even during our *us-and-theming*, it is possible to understand that the well-being of *my* grandchildren has intimate connection to the well-being of *their* grandchildren. We all live in a web of interdependent relationships that includes our enemies. And for many communities who have experienced sustained violence, the presence of those who threaten are not half a world away — they live next door.

While the horizon provides orientation, the daily path requires curiosity and courage.

In particular, we need curiosity about lived experience. We must become more curious about the inner landscape of suffering — of self and other — because here is where we find understanding about our behaviors, beliefs, actions, and reactions. Curiosity also nurtures the soil of where the seeds of courage and grace root.

Humanizing conflict requires us to curate a tender tenacity with an ability to hold to deeper truth while remaining open to new understanding and offering dignity for yourself and others. Dignity begins with the courage to embody curiosity.

Humanizing the face of conflict will always require two forms of courage to face down the toxicity of extreme polarization wielded to justify violence.

The first is the courage to reach beyond our narrow bubbles to open improbable conversation and hold fast to unlikely connections. Most of the stories shared in preceding chapters found people sitting and asking: Who do we know? How best do we take the first step beyond our circle of safety? Their strategy was never leaping from one mountain top to the other. It was always imagination of risk and the one step that could be taken today.

The second is the courage to face dehumanization, no matter its source or direction. This becomes exponentially more challenging when the source of dehumanization comes from your own group and is projected toward others. What matters most in tamping down extremism is not demanding that others change. It is the courage to humanize the other within our own group, to confront dehumanization when it appears close to home.

Combined, these two form the heart of social courage facing down toxicity. The stories shared in the preceding chapters exemplified this convergence: The courage to reach beyond safety and the refusal to dehumanize.

Humanizing the face of conflict is not a single act. It requires daily commitment, connections to others, and holding fast to relationships even when the pressures of polarization pull us apart.

INSIGHT 2
The Critical Yeast: The Power of the Improbable Few

The actions of an extreme few can easily harm the many. This happens when local pockets of violence develop connections, and connections create fluid but decentralized networks where violent ideas and action gain legitimacy, spawn, and spread. Once established, and often out of the purview of the wider public eye, even small events can mobilize surprisingly powerful reactions and outsized outcomes.

At the same time, innovative healing practices have roots that start local and often initiate with a few unusual relationships.

Facing down a civil war means that we must resist the tyranny of the extreme violent few by catalyzing the connective power of unlikely pockets of resistance. Even in small numbers wherever they live, people willing to reach beyond their inner circle and mobilize improbable relationships of sustained dialogue leading to joint action create the fabric that makes politics without violence possible and powerful.

Our gaze, perhaps overly directed by what mainstream journalism centers, does not naturally focus on these pockets of positive deviance. In fact, as noted, systems of toxicity live off finding ways to invisibilize alternatives or cynically deride them as unrealistic.

Often, the measure of value only assesses whether an idea or a movement has gained scale, whether movements have reached a critical mass. Value seems exclusively placed on scale at height and breadth — solutions that come from or impact high levels of political decision, or that have wide social impact. We have often missed what may matter most: Scale at *depth*.

Take our understanding of critical mass when applied to ideas or social movements. A journalist on the street might use the phrase critical mass to make a case for or against the significance of a movement by counting, for example, how many people are on the street at a protest. They focus on quantity.

If we look at physics and the origin of the term critical mass, the concept describes something different that quantity of production. The focus is on the *quality* of interaction.

Take the production of energy by way of nuclear chain reaction. In this context, critical mass references the point at which a *minimal* amount of fissile material *interacts* to *sustain* a chain reaction of energy output. The element of sustained is, in fact, critical. Stated differently, critical mass is the point at which the quality of interaction continues to produce energy independent of the originating catalyst. Critical mass attends less to the quantity than the *relational quality* needed to create a continuous flow of energy.

Let me repeat three key words: Minimal. Interacts. Sustains.

In all settings of armed conflict where people and politics resist violence, small pockets of unlikely relationships become interactive. Catalysts are present. Positive deviance spreads.

After decades of local work in settings of armed conflict, I have consistently found that the greatest innovations are rarely about large numbers. Rather, the transformative catalyst is the unexpected actions of the improbable few.

I refer to these pockets of vitality as the *critical yeast*.

In this metaphoric shift from nuclear energy to breadmaking, the smallest ingredient, when prepared and mixed, has the capacity to make everything else grow. It poses a central question for facing toxic polarization.

Who, if they act together across difference, can help everything else grow in a healthy direction?

Critical yeast focuses on quality of relationships — how they interact, find ways to connect, and engage across the diverse whole. This is tender tenacity at work. It is how people remain connected to their own convictions and community, while they choose to be in relationship with those who are different. In the face of adversity, together they propose specific ideas with the goal of shifting harmful patterns.

The varied contextual answers to this question in settings of armed conflict emerge with a strikingly similar pattern: Start small. Stay open to wider relationships. Learn to grow together. Propose. Act. Learn. Grow again.

INSIGHT 3
Accompaniment: Learning to Lead from Alongside

Across different initiatives, people seeking to face down toxic polarization learn to both walk together and nurture what is required to *stay together* across difference.

In settings of armed conflict, people never have the luxury of saying, *stop everything until we can sort this out.* Their challenge is how to break the cycles of violence while still living in them — an existential dilemma that makes complexity more a friend than enemy. This requires befriending people and sitting with conversations that offer insight into the very diverse stories and understandings that co-habit the social landscape surrounding conflict.

Complexity refuses binarism and will always pose the promise and challenge of accompaniment: How to lead from alongside? How to come alongside each other when our differences are not only about differences of political views, but about generational wounds?

I first learned the language and practices of accompaniment in the 1980s from Latin American colleagues. While the critical yeast offers a breadmaking metaphor, accompaniment — literally *with bread* in Latin — gives us the analogy of bread sharing.

Accompaniment means we must face the depth and harm of our different lived experiences, facing and acknowledging the historic wounds rooted exclusion and privilege. Being alongside requires us to find our way toward mutual dignity, repair, and inclusion amidst robust plurality. This is precisely what everyday people must navigate: Transforming legacies of harm incurred in the past as they face down the daily presence of violence.

Those who live in settings of armed conflict often find that the key to shifting toxicity requires a quality of leadership that comes alongside the fullness of experience, both lived and inherited. Leaders who accompany constructive change offer the courage to face overt social and political differences as well as the impacts of long histories of suffering. Coming alongside entails a practice that acknowledges the legacy of trauma and harm and at the same time engages immediate crises and differing views of how best to respond.

We carry a dominant image of leaders as visionaries, those who forge ahead cutting a path for others to follow. This certainly offers the power of example and prescience. At the same time, settings of wide-spread violence instruct us that the Mandelas of the world are few, and the waiting for the re-stitching of torn lives interminable.

As we discussed, a common dynamic in protracted conflict is leading from the wake. Leaders find themselves caught in the hostile pull of control and reactivity that replicates the very polarizing dynamics they themselves continue to unleash, with no horizon of meaningful change in sight.

The legacy of violence teaches us that when our wider social fabric is torn, its re-stitching will require us all. This weaving of social healing emerges through accompaniment attending to the well-being of individuals and the health of our relationships. To pursue social healing, we need to feel the embodied presence of courage and hope.

Facing down a civil war instructs us about the positive potential of pockets, this proximity of access and relationships that hold the promise of change. Alongside one another, people learn to weave the connective tissue needed to thread together the basic commitment that living *with* difference *without* violence is possible.

Final Words

Since 2016, the Colombian Truth Commission has sought to fulfill a mandate crafted in the peace accords that ended the country's longest standing armed conflict. As an advisor to the Commission, I had the extraordinary opportunity to watch their difficult work unfold, through COVID and through their long walk through the stories and corridors of more than fifty years of open war.

Those of us who study peace accords know that written agreements tend to suffer from rhetorical preludes followed by tedious descriptions of proposed actions.

The full title of the Commission embedded in the Colombian accord — *La Comisión para el Esclarecimiento de la Verdad, la Convivencia, y la No Repetición* — turned out to be an exception. So much so that the title defies rote translation from Spanish to English, perhaps begging for a more poetic rendering: *The Commission to Shed Light on Truth, Living Together, and Never Repeating Violence.*

Most official translations propose that their chosen word, *convivencia*, means "co-existence" — a rendering that deadens the very spirit of the concept.

The art of *convivencia* emerges in the habits and practices of living together.

Convivir suggests that *together* should be a verb fostering something akin to good neighborliness. Dignity respected. Belonging assured. Home secured.

The Commission's charge was not exclusively to offer a historic account of why patterns of violence repeated over a half century. They were tasked with shedding light — acknowledging victims' lived experience of harm — to clarify and unveil the pathways for living together in the fullness of human difference without violence.

John Avlon referred to a starkly similar moment in the United States in his book *Lincoln and the Fight for Peace*.[24] The core of the Colombian Commission's challenge seems proximate to Abraham Lincoln's Gettysburg words spoken in that precarious space between the just-lived scars of violence and the steps needed *to bind up the nation's wounds with malice toward none, with charity for all.*

What we may miss: The edge where wars end and the edge where wars begin are surprisingly similar.

Beginnings and endings. Both face the challenge of whether whole societies will slide, or back slide, into wide-spread open violence.

Lincoln's vision at the end of war offered the widest notion of shifting the whole of the body politic. His words and orientation not only sought to guide the United States back to shared humanity in the aftermath of war, but also to create common purpose that repairs harm. Lincoln's appeal was to redefine our relationships and transform the basic structures of society to shift legacies of exclusion and dehumanization toward inclusion and dignity. At its core, to align ourselves with the basic notion that all are created equal, all have a voice, and our greatest strength lies in how we create a politics of plurality. Lincoln's words underscore the belief that we can embody what sits on our coins: E pluribus unum. Out of many, one.

That appeal remains the exact challenge of how we face down toxicity at the edge of violence before a war starts.

Some will say the stories shared in *The Pocket Guide*, focused on ordinary people shifting patterns of violence, is a bit like the last sixty seconds of the evening news: One piece of hope shared to conclude the preceding thirty minutes of tragedy and loss. Nice but irrelevant.

I beg to differ.

The proportional inverse seems factually more accurate.

Even as I write, millions of people are *living into convivencia*, good neighborliness, far more than the number who choose spectacular displays of division and hatred. The question is how we stitch that potential. Together.

The Pocket Guide offers insight into how difficult it is to face down toxic polarization layered with violence and the surprising ways everyday people found to shift harmful patterns of violence that had lasted decades. This is only one part of a wider set of approaches and strategies for how we respond to the current challenges of historic divisions, political violence, and legacies harm in the United States. At the same time, I believe these exemplars from around the world can inspire a deeper reflection on how we bind our nation, heal wounds, and commit to politics without violence in our everyday lives.

Binding-and-healing, I suggest, requires that you watch your local pockets. *Where you live* is where you will find the people with the courage to reach beyond divisions and the perseverance to resist the push and pull of toxicity. When these pockets thread a web of creative resistance, they can face down a civil war.

I have not directly answered the question of whether we are being pulled to civil war in the United States.

Maybe that is not our question. It seems to cede far too much power to the tyranny of the extreme few whose lack of imagination mobilizes violence as the only remaining option.

I prefer the power of the improbable few, whose imagination mobilizes around the harder pathway of staying with relationships across difference that rehumanize with dignity and honesty.

A critical next step in this long and multifaceted journey of social healing is whether we will have the courage to nurture these pockets of vitality where we live that demonstrate a commitment to politics without violence as a daily practice.

In a nation of millions, facing down a civil war starts with each and every one of us.

Citations

[1] Elise Boulding, interview by Guy Burgess and Heidi Burgess, "What Exists Is Possible," *Beyond Intractability*, Conflict Information Consortium, University of Colorado, Boulder.

[2] *National Geographic*, "August 2001 Issue," August 2001.

[3] Debbie Uy, "Local Communities Push for Peace Zones," *Global Voices (blog)*, Institute for War & Peace Reporting, February 21, 2020.

[4] *Pray the Devil Back to Hell*, directed by Gini Reticker (Fork Films, 2008).

[5] Donna Hicks, *Dignity: Its Essential Role in Resolving Conflict* (New Haven, CT: Yale University Press, 2011).

[6] Bruno Bettelheim, *Violence as a Mode of Behavior in the Individual*, manuscript, 1964.

[7] Vamik D. Volkan, "Transgenerational Transmissions and Chosen Traumas: An Aspect of Large-Group Identity," *Group Analysis* 34, no. 1 (2001): 79-97, https://doi.org/10.1177/05333160122077730.

[8] Conciliation Resources, "In Memoriam: Brendan McAllister (1956–2022)," December 2022.

[9] Tanenbaum, "Meet the Peacemakers: Ricardo Esquivia Ballestas," January 2024.

[10] Comisión de la Verdad, "Francisco José de Roux"

[11] Comisión de la Verdad, https://www.comisiondelaverdad.co/.

[12] Seamus Heaney, "Whatever You Say, Say Nothing," in *Selected Poems, 1966-1987** (London: Faber and Faber, 1990), 54.

[13] Trade for Peace, "Building a Legacy: Women's Empowerment in South Sudan," hosted by Axel M. Addy, featuring Rose Acindhel Kacthiek, podcast audio, released September 14, 2022.

[14] Lada Adamic and Natalie Glance, "The Political Blogosphere and the 2004 U.S. Election: Divided They Blog," *Proceedings of the 3rd International Workshop on Link Discovery* (2005): 36-43.

[15] Diálogos Improbables, https://dialogoimprobable.org/.

[16] Natural Resource Conflict Transformation Center-Nepal, https://nrctc.org.np/.

[17] Nelson Mandela, "Inaugural Address by President Nelson Mandela," delivered at the Union Buildings, Pretoria, South Africa, May 10, 1994, South African Government News Agency.

[18] *Invictus,* directed by Clint Eastwood (Burbank, CA: Warner Bros. Pictures, 2009).

[19] Centro Nacional de Memoria Histórica, *Un bosque de memoria viva: Desde la Alta Montaña de El Carmen de Bolívar* (Bogotá: Centro Nacional de Memoria Histórica, 2018).

[20] Asvidas María Labaja, https://asvidasmarialabaja.weebly.com/.

[21] Universidad de los Andes, "Juana Alicia Ruiz," *Historias de Vida.*

[22] Gerald M. Edelman, *Remembered Present: A Biological Theory of Consciousness,* 1st ed. (New York: The Overlook Press, 2008).

[23] Seamus Heaney, *The Cure at Troy* (New York: Farrar, Straus, and Giroux, 1990).

[24] John Avlon, *Lincoln and the Fight for Peace* (New York: Simon & Schuster, 2019).

Further Reading and Resources

To access a free PDF of *The Pocket Guide*, visit:
www.johnpaullederach.com/pocket-guide

Additional Readings from John Paul Lederach

For greater elaboration of many of the stories shared in *The Pocket Guide*, please reference:
  The Moral Imagination: The Art and Soul of Building Peace

Additional books and essays by John Paul Lederach that engage the themes of *The Pocket Guide* include:
  Adam Curle: Radical Peacemaker by Tom Woodhouse and John Paul Lederach

  "Mediating Conflict in Central America" by Paul Wehr and John Paul Lederach

  Memoirs of Nepal: Reflections Across a Decade

  "The Challenge of Terror: A Traveling Essay"

  The Little Book of Conflict Transformation: Clear Articulation of the Guiding Principles by a Pioneer in the Field

  "The Long Journey Back to Humanity: Catholic Peacebuilding with Armed Actors" in *Peacebuilding: Catholic Theology, Ethics, and Praxis*, edited by Robert J. Schreiter, Scott R. Appleby, and Gerard F. Powers

  The Poetic Unfolding of the Human Spirit

  "Resiliency and Healthy Communities: An Exploration of Image and Metaphor"

  When Blood and Bones Cry Out: Journeys Through the Soundscape of Healing and Reconciliation by John Paul Lederach and Angela Jill Lederach

Further Reading by Chapter

FOREWORD

High Conflict: Why We Get Trapped and How We Get Out by Amanda Ripley

How Civil Wars Start: And How to Stop Them by Barbara F. Walter

CHAPTER 1: Watch Your Pockets

The story of the Women of Wajir can be seen via the documentary entitled, "The Wajir Story." See also, *Mediation and Governance in Fragile Contexts: Small Steps to Peace* by Dekha Ibrahim Abdi and Simon J.A. Mason

Politics Is about Relationship: A Blueprint for the Citizens' Century by Harold H. Saunders

CHAPTER 2: Hiding in Plain Sight

Democracies Divided: The Global Challenge of Political Polarization edited by Thomas Carothers and Andrew O'Donohue

Hijos de la violencia: Campesinos de Colombia sobreviven a "golpes" de paz by Alejandro Garcia

Mighty Be Our Powers: How Sisterhood, Prayer, and Sex Changed a Nation at War by Leymah Gbowee and Carol Mithers

"Ten ideas on how to overcome polarization" by Mark Freeman and Hilary Pennington

The Way Out: How to Overcome Toxic Polarization by Peter T. Coleman

Why We're Polarized by Ezra Klein

CHAPTER 3: The Holy Grail of Grievance

"A Review and Provocation: On Polarization and Platforms" by Daniel Kreiss and Shannon C. McGregor

Breaking Intergenerational Cycles of Repetition: A Global Dialogue on Historical Trauma and Memory edited by Pumla Gobodo-Madikizela

Dignity: Its Essential Role in Resolving Conflict by Donna Hicks

The Little Book of Trauma Healing: When Violence Strikes and Community Security Is Threatened by Carolyn Yoder

"Toward a Theory of Pernicious Polarization and How It Harms Democracies: Comparative Evidence and Possible Remedies" by Jennifer McCoy and Murat Somer

When the Center Does Not Hold: Leading in an Age of Polarization by David R. Brubaker

CHAPTER 4: The Rituals of Fear

"Northern Reticence: Articulating a Culture of Silence in Northern Ireland" by Leszek Drong

Say Nothing: A True Story of Murder and Memory in Northern Ireland by Patrick Radden Keefe

"'Silence is the Mother of All Wars' but They 'Didn't Respect the Law of Silence'" by Paola Desiderio

Standing at the Edge: Finding Freedom Where Fear and Courage Meet by Joan Halifax

CHAPTER 5: The 90% Rule

An Improbable Friendship: The Remarkable Lives of Israeli Ruth Dayan and Palestinian Raymonda Tawil and Their Forty-Year Peace Mission by Anthony David

Bridges across an Impossible Divide: The Inner Lives of Arab and Jewish Peacemakers by Marc Gopin

"Democracy Narratives and Sacred Values" from the Horizons Project and the Alliance for Peacebuilding

Narrative, Power, and Polarisation: The Role of Influential Actors from the Institute for Integrated Transitions

The Neutrality Trap: Disrupting and Connecting for Social Change by Bernard S. Mayer and Jacqueline N. Font-Guzmán

"Sacred Values, Willingness to Sacrifice, and Accountability for the Capitol Insurrection: Exploring How Deeply and Why Americans Hold Their January 6 Related Views" by Over Zero, New America, and Project Democracy

"The Role of Narrative in Managing Conflict and Supporting Peace" from the Institute for Integrated Transitions

CHAPTER 6: Growth by Fractions

"The Science of Polarization and Insights for Bridge-building" by Nichole Argo Ben Itzhak

CHAPTER 7: It Only Takes One

Beautiful Souls: The Courage and Conscience of Ordinary People in Extraordinary Times by Eyal Press

Long Walk to Freedom by Nelson Mandela

Small Acts of Courage: A Legacy of Endurance and the Fight for Democracy by Ali Velshi

Small Acts of Resistance: How Courage, Tenacity, and Ingenuity Can Change the World by Steve Crawshaw and John Jackson

CHAPTER 8: The Mapping of Where There Be Dragons

Feel the Grass Grow: Ecologies of Slow Peace in Colombia by Angela Jill Lederach

"How Memory Can Help Heal Trauma — From Colombia to Chicago" by Laura Zornosa

"'Making Memory': Historical Memory in Colombia and Its Legacies" by María del Rosario Acosta López

"Old world new times: exploring contested language in a post conflict society" by Duncan Morrow and Jonny Byrne

Second Nature: Brain Science and Human Knowledge by Gerald Edelman

The Depolarizing of America: A Guidebook for Social Healing by Kirk J. Schneider

CHAPTER 9: Leading from the Wake

Claiming the Courageous Middle: Daring to Live and Work Together for a More Hopeful Future by Shirley A. Mullen

How to Have Impossible Conversations: A Very Practical Guide by Peter Boghossian and James Lindsay

I Never Thought of It That Way: How to Have Fearlessly Curious Conversations in Dangerously Divided Times by Mónica Guzmán

Moral Tribes: Emotion, Reason, and the Gap Between Us and Them by Joshua Greene

CHAPTER 10: Drawing Lines

Belonging: The Science of Creating Connection and Bridging Divides by Geoffrey L. Cohen

Belonging without Othering: How We Save Ourselves and the World by john a. powell and Stephen Menendian

Possible: How We Survive (and Thrive) in an Age of Conflict by Bill Ury

CONCLUSIONS

Defusing American Anger: A Guide to Understanding our Fellow Citizens and Reducing Us-vs-Them Polarization by Zachary Elwood

"Dehumanization and the Normalization of Violence: It's Not What You Think" by Aliza Luft

Everyday Peace: How So-called Ordinary People Can Disrupt Violent Conflict by Roger Mac Ginty

The Next American Revolution: Sustainable Activism for the Twenty-First Century by Grace Lee Boggs with Scott Kurashige

The Frontlines of Peace: An Insider's Guide to Changing the World by Séverine Autesserre

Get Involved

If you are looking to find ways to get involved in your community, here are some resources you might explore.

Organizational Directories

- *America's Healthy Democracy Ecosystem Project* from the National Civic League (while this ecosystem map is not yet public, you are welcome to reach out to the National Civic League for more information)
- *Citizen Connect* from the Bridge Alliance
- *Building Resilience Ecosystem Map* from the Bridging Divides Initiative
- *De-Escalation Directory* from the Bridging Divides Initiative
- *#ListenFirst Coalition*
- *Peacebuilding Starts at Home* from the Alliance for Peacebuilding (please reference Effort 2)
- *TRUST Partners* of the TRUST Network
- *Truth, Racial Healing, and Transformation Movement Organizations* from the Bridging Divides Initiative
- *Weave Community*
- *Welcoming Network* from Welcoming America

University Campus Initiatives

- *BridgeUSA*
- *Constructive Dialogue Institute*
- *Interfaith America*
- *Sustained Dialogue Institute*

Training Resources

- *Bridging Differences Playbook* from the Greater Good Science Center

- *Connection Hub* from the Einhorn Collaborative

- *Cultivating Contact: A Guide to Building Bridges and Meaningful Connections Between Groups* from Welcoming America, the Center for Inclusion and Belonging, and the University of Massachusetts Amherst

- *Harnessing Our Power to End Political Violence* from The Horizons Project and 22nd Century Initiative

- *How to Have Authentic Relational Conversations* from the United Vision Project

- *Peacemaker's Toolkit: A Reference Guide for Reconciliation in Your Community* from Search for Common Ground

- *Specialized Briefing Guides & Toolkits* from Over Zero

- *Resonant* from Bedrock

- *Toolkit for Constructive Dialogue in Polarized Contexts* by the Institute for Integrated Transitions

About the Author

John Paul Lederach is Professor Emeritus at the University of Notre Dame and a Senior Fellow with Humanity United. He works extensively as a practitioner in local and national peace processes with extensive experience in Latin America, Africa, Southeast and Central Asia, and Europe. Lederach is widely known for the development of culturally based approaches to conflict transformation and the design and implementation of integrative and strategic approaches to peacebuilding. He is author and co-editor of 30 books and manuals, including *Building Peace: Sustainable Reconciliation in Divided Societies* (USIP Press), *The Little Book of Conflict Transformation* (Skyhorse Publishing), and *The Moral Imagination: The Art and Soul of Building Peace* (Oxford University Press).

Learn more about John Paul Lederach and his contributions to the fields of peacebuilding and conflict transformation by visiting: www.johnpaullederach.com.